ORAL COMMUNICATION

FIRST EDITION

ORAL COMMUNICATION

A LECTURE GUIDE

GAIL-ANN GREAVES-VENZEN, PH.D.
Long Island University, Brooklyn Campus

Bassim Hamadeh, *CEO and Publisher*

John Remington, *Executive Editor*

Tony Paese, *Project Editor*

Berenice Quirino, *Associate Production Editor*

Jess Estrella, *Senior Graphic Designer*

Danielle Gradisher, *Licensing Associate*

Natalie Piccotti, *Director of Marketing*

Kassie Graves, *Vice President of Editorial*

Jamie Giganti, *Director of Academic Publishing*

Printed in *the United States of America.*

ISBN: 978-1-5165-2974-2 *(pbk) / 978-1-5165-2975-9 (br)*

CONTENTS

CHAPTER 1

Introduction to Communication

"I am a good Communicator. I am in control of my thoughts, words, and actions. I only think, speak, and act in ways that create and fulfill the best in me!"

—Dr. Shad Helmstetter

Point of Reference

The gas company dug up the sidewalk in front of the house to install new gas pipes. The next morning, as I was talking my six year old to school, she saw the mess and hole in the sidewalk. Immediately she stated, "I can't believe this! They made a mess! Look at this mess, mommy. They did not clean it up!" As we drove off in the car, still upset by the hole in the sidewalk, she exclaimed: "They need to go back to school and learn how to do it correctly. They need to go back to Kindergarten and learn." I smiled as I questioned: "Kindergarten?" "Yes, mommy. Kindergarten," she said, proud to be a first grader. It dawned on me, "Yes Kindergarten." It made sense to her because that was her point of reference. She was in first grade. Although she knew that one day she would attend university, she could only provide meaning based on her limited experiences. What is your point of reference? How does your point of reference affect the way in which you communicate and interpret messages? Too often we rush to judgment because we attach our meaning to others' messages without understanding their point of reference. Before we dive into how to become dynamic presenters, we must first understand what makes us effective communicators. To be a dynamic presenter, you must be an effective communicator by understanding your role and the role of the audience during the communication process.

What is Communication?

What is communication? What are some ways in which we communicate? If you thought that we communicate through talking, texting, emails, signs, advertisements, body language, facial expressions, eye contact, singing, dance, art, clothing, smoke signal, smelling, etc., you are right. Are you an effective communicator? If yes, then what makes you an effective communicator? These are some of the questions we will address in this chapter. In addition, we will clear up some misconceptions you may have about communication.

Communication is a process in which we share and understand ideas. The definition is a very simple one for such a complicated process. At a quick glance, communication seems simple. But is it? Initially, your definition of communication might have only focused on the written or spoken messages. There are, however, many other elements to consider.

To further understand the definition of communication let us define all the keywords in our previous definition of communication.

The first significant word in our definition is a **process**. What is a process? Merriam-Webster.com (2015) defines the process as "a series of actions that produce something or that lead to a particular result." How does this definition fit into your ideas of communication? Let us go a little deeper in our definition of a process and equate communication to the process of baking a cake. Even if you have never baked a cake, you can easily picture the steps involved in the process.

TABLE 1.1 **Communication as a Process of Baking a Cake**

Cake	Communication
Ingredients	Elements
Tools	Five senses
Recipe	Theories
Mix together	Communication is dynamic and irreversible
Put in oven and wait	Communication occurs within a given context and time
Take the cake out of the oven	Input and outcomes

The first step in baking a cake is to gather your needed **ingredients**: eggs, milk, flour, water, sugar, etc. The ingredients required to communicate are called elements (Berlo, 1960): sender, receiver, channel, message, noise, context, encode, decode. These elements are dependent on one another. The second step in our process of baking a cake is to gather your tools: pans, bowls, spoons, etc. The tools needed to communicate are your **five senses**: see, hear, taste, smell, and touch.

It is easy to understand how you communicate through seeing with your eyes and hearing with your ears. But how do you use your other senses to communicate? Let us examine **touch**. In the United States business world, the handshake is one method of recognition. But do you know how the handshake originated? In the article "What is the origin of the Handshake?" Evan Andrews explains that it began as a way of conveying peaceful intentions. "Strangers extended empty right hands to show that they did not have weapons and bore no ill will toward one another, and the up-and-down motion of the handshake was supposed to dislodge any knives or daggers that might be hidden up a sleeve" (Evan Andrews, 2016). Today, the handshake can symbolize good faith when closing a deal. It is a symbol of power. If the handshake is too weak, it indicates that the individual is insecure. Likewise, if the handshake is too strong, it suggests that the person is trying to overcompensate. When go on a job interview, wait until the interviewer offers to shake your hand because you do not want to step into the interview's personal space unless invited. If the interviewer offers to shake your hand as you approach him or her, look the interviewer in the eye and say, "Good morning, [their title and name.] My name is ... and I am here to interview for ... position. It is a pleasure to meet you." Remember to give a good handshake where you grasp the entire hand and squeeze in a firm but non-aggressive manner. Web must meet web, and palm must meet palm before gripping. No grabbing of the fingers or limp handshake. In a study conducted by Stewart, Dustin, Barrick, & Darnold (2008), it was found that the "quality of handshake was related to interviewer hiring recommendations." However, if the interviewer does not offer his or her hand, do not offer yours, as this action might be due to culture, gender, or personal preferences. You do not want to start the interview by putting your interviewer in an awkward position of having to explain his or herself. Simply greet the interviewer, and wait for his or her directive. Factors such as culture, profession, and gender can also influence the meaning of the handshake.

Human beings need touch. To feel secure, we self-touch and allow others to touch us. Touch is so important that hospitals have volunteers and staff members who hold abandoned babies or babies whose parents cannot visit frequently. Parents are encouraged to Kangaroo Mother Care (KMC) premature babies. Kangaroo Mother Care is a process where a parent holds the newborn baby skin to skin on the chest. It decreases stress in mothers of premature babies and increases infants' ability to make requests and respond to parental interaction (Suman Rao et al., 2008). In addition, KMC decreases neonatal deaths in pre-term birth complications (Sloan, Ahmed, Anderson, & Moore, 2011). When my daughter was born at 28 weeks, and weighed 3 pounds 4 ounces, the nurses in the NICU encouraged us to touch and kangaroo care her daily to enhance her development.

As with touch, **smell** is another tool we use to communicate. If you take milk from the refrigerator for your cereal and **see** that the expiration date has passed, what do you do next? You *smell* it. Our nose alerts us to dangerous gas or to pleasant scents of fine cuisine. We can also communicate attraction and emotions through smell. In order to investigate if human beings, like animals, communicate their emotional states through changes in body odor, researchers (Chen & Haviland-Jones, 2000) collected underarm odors from 25 young women and men who watched a funny movie on one day and a frightening movie on another. A week later, they found that 40 women and 37 men were able to identify "the odor of people when they are happy," and "the odor of people when they are afraid."

Since emotions are communicated through smell, you should not wear perfume or cologne when you go on a job interview. Why? There is something called smell recognition. Have you ever smelled a particular scent and automatically thought about someone you knew? Wearing perfume or cologne is almost like playing Russian roulette, and for two reasons: The interviewer may be allergic to the scent, or if the smell reminds the interviewer of someone he or she dislikes, then that feeling will be transferred to you the interviewee. Newborn babies use smell to identify their mothers. One trick I used with my newborn daughter was to leave the blouse I was wearing in her crib when I needed to go out. It gave her the feeling that I was near her.

While communication through smell is interesting, just how do we communicate through taste? Taste helps us enjoy the flavor of our food or lets us know whether it has gone sour. It is reported that Thomas Edison would offer potential research assistant candidates a bowl of soup during an interview. If they seasoned it with salt and pepper before tasting it, he would disqualify them. Why? What do you think seasoning your food before tasting it indicates about the person? If you guess that they are judgmental, you would be correct. Edison wanted assistants who would not make assumptions (Jeff Haden, 2018). If we go back to the example of the milk, after you smell it, you then taste it to make sure it has not gone sour before pouring it on the cereal.

MISCONCEPTION #1: Communication is just speaking. This is not the case. Communication includes everything. Your five senses are always activated. Silence is a form of communication. You can say a lot by not saying anything. Have you ever had someone become upset with you, and you did not mention anything? But the individual might have seen something in your eyes or facial expressions that indicated to him or her that you were upset. Remember that communication is not just talking; everything you do encompasses some form of communication

The third step in the process of baking our cake is to mix all the ingredients. What you need to understand is that communication is dynamic (Samovar & Porter, 1988), meaning that communication changes and evolves. Just as the cake ingredients when mixed changes, so do the elements of communication. Once you mixed the cake ingredients their form changed and you can no longer see the eggs, milk, sugar, etc. Likewise, when the elements of communication interact with one another, the elements and the process change. You can never communicate the same way twice. Some of you are now probably saying, "NO, I can communicate the same way twice." Notice I did not state that you couldn't send the same message twice, but rather that you cannot communicate the same way twice. This means the process of communication can never be repeated the same way. Why? The reason is that communication is *dynamic*. You might say the same message twice. For example, you might say, "Go outside." If I asked you to repeat what you said, you would repeat the same message or words. But would you use the same tone of voice, facial expression, and body language, etc.? Is the environment or time the same? And are the thought processes of the people communicating the same? Of course not! In addition, communication is irreversible. Once you mix the ingredients and they change forms, you cannot undo the change. So with communication, once you send a message you cannot take it back. Be careful when you send emails or text messages to someone. You cannot "unsend" them, and they are permanent records that can be used against you in the future.

The fourth step in the process of baking the cake is to place the mixture in the oven and wait. Communication occurs within a given context and time. For instance, while in the context of the doctor's office, you expect your doctor to touch your body when performing a physical examination. In the context of the office setting, however, it would be inappropriate for your boss to feel your body, even if he or she is a doctor. In the latter context, it would be considered sexual harassment. If you were taking this class online, it would be appropriate for you to wear pajamas and put your feet up on the chair in the context of your house. But if you were in the context of the classroom, these actions would be considered inappropriate.

The fifth step in our process is to take the cake out the oven. There are inputs and outcomes to our communication. If you input the information effectively by considering your audience, you will get the right result.

The second key word in our definition of communication is sharing. What is sharing? Do not say the trademark of the Salvation Army "sharing is caring." Ever watch a group of year-old toddlers trying to share? Rather, sharing is the giving and receiving of messages. For us to communicate, we must share ideas. But what if you are alone? How are you then sharing? You are communicating with yourself through a process called intrapersonal communication. We will discuss that concept later in this chapter.

Finally, how would you define understanding ideas? Is your definition to know what someone is saying or to be able to explain ideas clearly? The definition of *understanding ideas* is to provide meaning for the message. Everyone provides meaning and everyone provides meaning differently. This is the reason why we communicate ineffectively—we tend to use our point of reference when defining other messages.

MISCONCEPTION #2: Most people believe the meaning is in the words. But meaning is NOT in the words but rather in the individual. Yes, we have dictionary meaning for words; however, five factors determine how we apply meaning to the messages and words. You provide meaning for messages based on your experiences, culture, emotions, environment, and physiological makeup.

Providing Meaning

How do you provide the meaning for the messages we receive? There are five basic factors that impact how we perceive messages and understand the world we live in. These five factors determine our point of reference. The first factor that determines our point of reference is past experiences. Your experiences determine how you perceive the world. You are a sum of your experiences. How so? Let us say you are in a relationship and everything is going well. One day your partner announces that he or she is going to *hang out with friends on Friday nights*. After a couple of months, you learn that your partner was cheating on you. You break off the relationship and move on. You start a new relationship, and everything is going well. Then one day your new partner announces that he or she will be *hanging out with friends on Friday nights*. What do you think? You are probably thinking that your partner will cheat on you. Unless you discuss your views with your partner, your definition of the words *hang out with friends on Friday nights* will cause a rift in your relationship. You will have arguments and fights over minor issues, but the underlying cause of the arguments is the unresolved issues of those words *hang out with friends on Friday nights*.

The second factor is our culture. Our culture has an enormous effect on how we perceive messages and the world (Hall, 1959, 1966). It defines who we are as individuals. Culture is defined as "the manifold ways of perceiving and organizing the world that are held in common by a group of people and passed on interpersonally and intergenerationally." (Hecht, Andersen, Ribeau, 1989 p. 163) It includes our language, religion, beliefs, values, attitudes, knowledge, experiences, roles, etc. Messages can have different meanings depending on someone's culture. In the United States, people view the peace sign as something positive. But in some countries, such as Australia and England, the backward peace sign is a derogatory gesture. In Latin America and sub-Saharan Africa, it's okay to arrive late for a social event, whereas in Germany and Switzerland arriving late would be considered rude. Most people believe that individuals who migrate to the United States assimilate to U.S. culture—the melting pot theory. But sociologist Milton Gordon (1976) described three models of assimilation in the United States: Anglo-conformity, the melting pot, and cultural pluralism. The term *cultural pluralism*—when smaller groups within a larger society maintain their unique cultural identities—best describes what is occurring when individuals migrate to the United States. Today it is not unusual to find pockets of cultures in different areas within a cultural village. When individuals leave the cultural village to go to school or work, they do not leave their cultural norms or practices behind. Sometimes disagreements at school or work may be due to cultural differences. In African American and Caribbean cultures it is disrespectful for a child to look an adult in the eyes when being disciplined. In most Eurocentric cultures, however, the child should look at the adult to show respect. It is important to learn about a culture before visiting another country so that you do not inadvertently send the wrong message.

The third factor that influences how we perceive messages are our emotions. Our emotions determine how we perceive our world, organize our memory, and make important decisions. In the article "5 Ways Your Emotions Influence Your World," Stephanie Pappas (2014) provides results from 5 major studies that revealed 1) that being in love makes food and drinks taste sweeter; 2) that giving an interviewer a heavy clipboard can make them think job candidates are more serious; 3) that people with a weak physical pose feel powerless and perceive items as heavier; 4) that lonely people have a stronger perception of cold; and 5) that holding a warm beverage makes people see stranger as warmer and more friendly. If you ride the train during rush hour in New York City, you become accustomed to people being in close proximity. But if you are not feeling well or are upset, you tend to hate everything, including the train, the people, your job, etc. Same experience but two different emotions can lead to two distinct meanings. Therefore, you should not make major decisions when you are emotional. My father, a detective, always said there are a lot of people in jail because of emotion. For instance, you get into an argument with someone. You hit the individual, and he or she falls, hits his or her head, and dies. Now you are headed to prison for manslaughter. Before I left the hospital with my daughter, my husband and I were required to view the shaken baby syndrome video. The hospital also advised us that if we ever felt stressed because the baby was continuously crying, to then walk away and let her cry rather than deal with her while we were emotional. Hospitals are being proactive because most people do not know that shaking a baby to stop it from crying causes permanent brain damage or even death.

Our environment is the fourth factor that determines how we perceive messages. When you enter the classroom, your professors expect you to come to the class properly dressed, to sit up, and to take notes. If you were taking the class online, however, you might be lying in bed in your pajamas watching TV or even texting. Have you ever gone to a party and arrived either underdressed or overdressed? How did that make you feel? You might have left because you felt uncomfortable.

Our physiological makeup determines how we perceive messages. Your age, agenda, ethnicity, height, hair color, body type, etc., all determine how you view messages. I am 5 feet 3 inches tall, but I grew up in a family where everyone was tall. My father and brother were both 6 feet and my mother 5 feet 8 inches. I took after the ladies on my dad's side of the family, who were short. The short jokes are not funny to me. You must be careful when you're making jokes about people's physical characteristics. They are NOT politically correct, and you could be creating unknown enemies.

It is important to understand that when you are communicating with someone, all five of these factors are influencing you both. Therefore, you have to take time to understand your receiver(s).

MISCONCEPTION #3: Most people believe that if someone disagrees with them or provides a different meaning to their message, there was no communication. But this is false! Remember, you are always communicating because you are always sharing and understanding ideas.

The Process of Communication

In the process of communication, a sender encodes or formulates a message and sends it through a particular channel(s) to the receiver, who decodes the message and encodes a feedback message to the sender, who in turn decodes the feedback message. Within the communication process, there is noise that prevents the communication from being effective. The process occurs within a given context. This is the theoretical explanation of the process of communication.

In the past, communication was thought to be *linear*, meaning that a sender sent a message to the receiver.

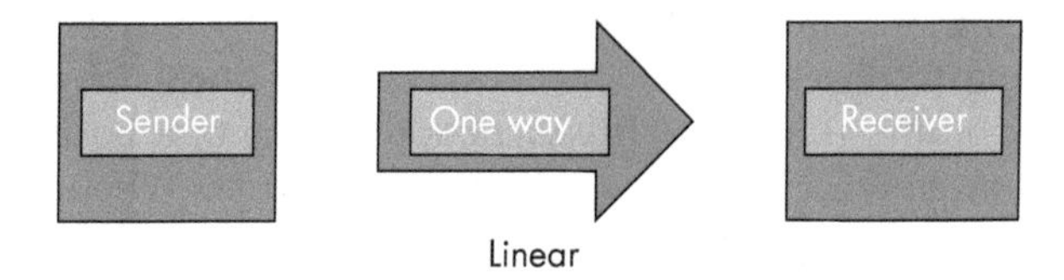

FIGURE 1.1.

Linear

In 1948, mathematician Claude Elwood Shannon developed and published the first linear model for communication.

But this was later changed when David Berlo expanded this linear model to an interactive the Sender-Message-Channel-Receiver (SMCR) Model of Communication. He realized that the linear view did not include the receiver's response or feedback and context. His model also included the 5 senses of human perception as channels in the process.

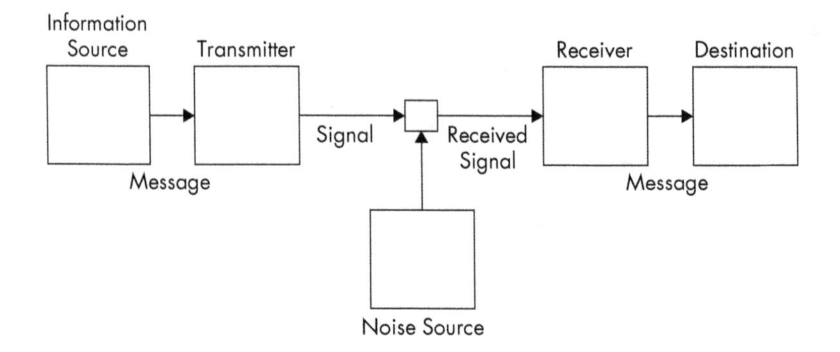

FIGURE 1.2. Shannon Model of Communication

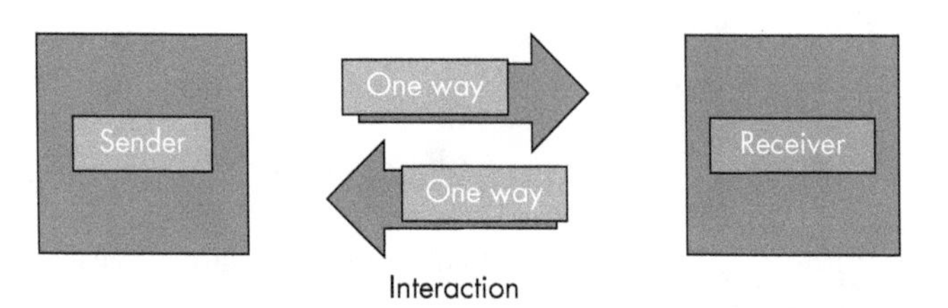

FIGURE 1.3.

Interaction

Although these models gave us an understanding on how we communicate, they were too simple. Thanks to the efforts of Wilbur Schramm (1954), whose model included the encoding, decoding, feedback, and the McCroskey Model (1968), which include noise, today we regard communication as *transaction*, meaning that both the sender and receiver are sending and receiving messages at the same time. When you put together all the theories, the process looks like the following diagram.

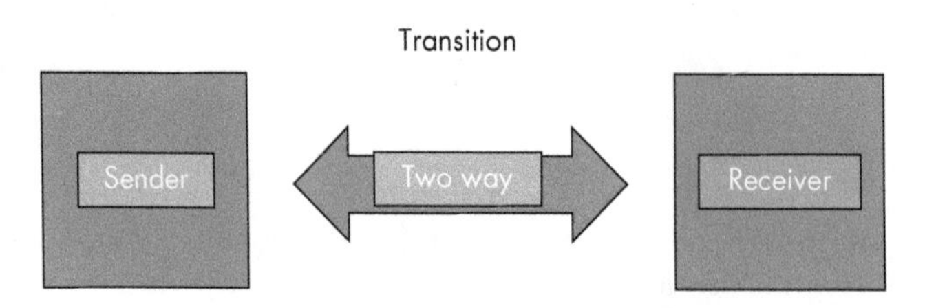

FIGURE 1.4.

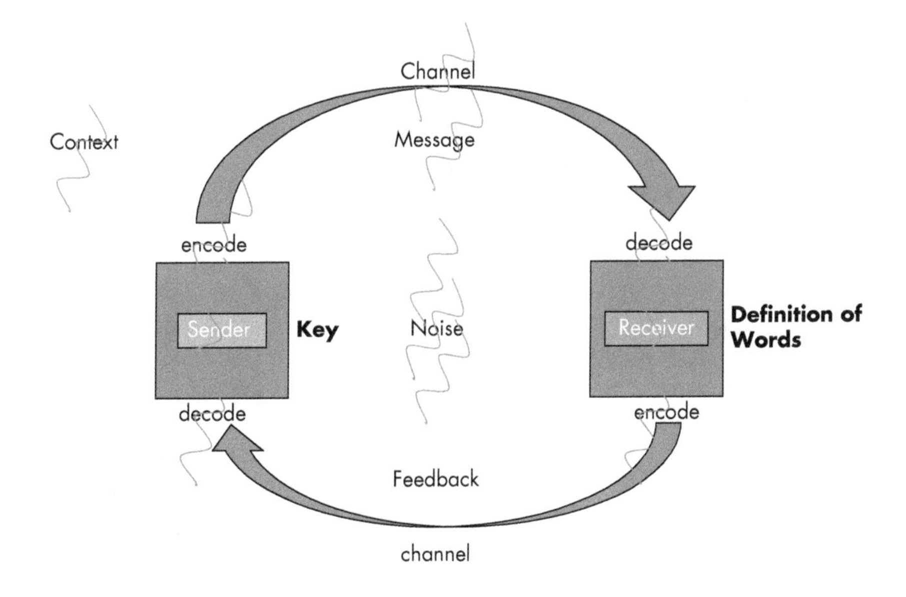

FIGURE 1.5.

The sender is the person who starts or initiates the process. We are all senders of messages. Sometimes the message is sent intentionally and other times unintentionally. The message is sent intentionally when we consciously encode it. If you are going to a day party and access Pinterest to see what people are wearing at day parties, then you are intentionally sending the message. But sometimes through our nonverbal messages, we do not intentionally mean to send messages—but we do. If you make a disgusted facial expression while you mother is scolding you, but it was not your intention to communicate this feeling, then your messages were sent unintentionally.

Encoding is the formulating or putting together of the message. There is a time factor involved when you are encoding the message. When you are engaged in a conversation, you tend to encode messages quickly; however, if you are sending an email or writing a paper, the encoding process is longer. The more relevant the message, the more time we take to encode it.

The channel is the audio or visual pathway used to transmit the message. The message is the idea you are communicating. The message can be verbal, which is communication through words, languages, or symbols, or nonverbal, which is communication through actions not through words, languages, or symbols.

Verbal vs. Nonverbal Communication

Most people confuse *verbal* communication with *vocal* communication. Therefore, to be considered verbal communication they think the message has to be spoken. This view is false. The message could be spoken or written. What are some examples of verbal communication? Texting, emails, signs, books, etc., are all examples of verbal messages. If you send a text to your friend to meet you at 5 p.m. and your friend meets you at 5 p.m., then you sent the message through verbal communication. Once the message comes from the language, the words, or the symbols, it is verbal communication. What about sign language? Is it verbal or nonverbal communication? Most of you will probably answer nonverbal communication because the individuals are using their hands to communicate. But since the messages are coming from the symbols, then sign language is a form of verbal communication.

Nonverbal communication is based on actions. So what are some examples of nonverbal communication? Facial expressions, body language, eye contact, artifacts, etc., are all forms of nonverbal communication. Does the voice carry elements of nonverbal communication? Yes, it does. How so? Through your tone, rate, pitch, volume, articulation, and pronunciation the voice communicates nonverbal messages. It is not what you say but how you say it. Have you ever had a friend tell you during a phone conversation that he or she is okay but you perceived that something was wrong? The message that *something was wrong* came through nonverbal communication, called paralanguage.

Which do you think is more effective—your verbal messages or nonverbal messages? Most people are tempted to say verbal communication. Nonverbal communication, however, has more effect than verbal communication; 55%–66% of your communication comes from nonverbal sources, and if you add vocal communications that percentage jumps to 85%–90%. If there is a contradiction between verbal and nonverbal messages, people tend to believe your nonverbal communication. Have you ever heard the saying, "Actions speaks louder than words"? People look to your nonverbal messages for clarification. For instance, on an employment interview you are asked whether you work well under pressure. If you reply "yes" but your hands and voice are shaking, the interviewer will not believe your words.

The **receiver** is the person who decodes the sender's message and provides feedback to the sender. **Decoding** occurs when the sender or receiver interprets or provides meaning for the message received. **Feedback** is the verbal or nonverbal response to the sender's message. It is vital to ensure that communication is effective.

One of the reasons why communication is ineffective is due to **noise**. Noise, not to be confused with sound, is anything that interferes with the process. There is always noise in the communication process. It is a part of every element. We cannot get rid of the noise, but as a communicator our goal is to minimize the noise. There are three types of noises. **Internal** is the psychological and physiological interferences in the communication process. For instance, if before you go to school you had an argument with one of your parents, when you get to school it would be difficult to concentrate on the professor's lecture. You would probably focus more on the argument than on the lecture. To minimize the noise, you should take good notes that you can review later. An example of physiological noise would be a stomachache or headache that prevents you from concentrating on the lecture.

External noise refers to the physical conditions surrounding you that interfere with the communication process. For example, if while your professor is lecturing it begins to rain heavily, your focus will now be on getting home and not on the professor's lecture. As a speaker, it is important to consider external noise. At my graduation, the speaker was on a covered dais while the graduates, friends, and families sat in the open. A plane began to skywrite the message, "Will you marry me?" Once the skywriter added the name, everyone began to cheer, and the speaker thought we were applauding her, but we were more focused on reading the message and looking for the program to find the individual. If the room temperature is too hot or too cold or the light is too bright or too dark, it would be difficult for the audience to focus on the lecturer or speaker.

External communication noise can be a microphone squeaking, your PowerPoint being too small, or protesters making noise outside the building.

Semantic deals with how we define the words that we use. For instance, someone might say, "You look PHAT/fat." But did the person compliment or insult you? Remember, we said earlier that the meaning is not in the words but in the individual. When people are about to get married, it is recommended that they receive marriage counseling. Why? Because your definition of marriage is based on what you have seen. If your definition of marriage conflicts with your partner's definition of marriage, then chances are there will be problems within the marriage. When someone uses the word *love*, is he or she defining the term the same as you? I tell my three-year-old daughter all the time that I love her, and she responds in kind; however, our definition of love is different from each other. Does she understand what love is? She probably defines love as happiness. When she grows older, and she experiences more in life, she will change her definition of love. It is important to understand how people are defining the words they use. To be an effective communicator you cannot assume that someone is defining words similar to you. You must always take the time to understand the other person's definition. It is good to ask the question: What do you mean?

The context is the type, time, and place where the communication process occurs. As I mentioned earlier, your meaning to a particular message might be different depending on the context.

Effective Communication

To communicate effectively, what should be your primary focus? No, it is not the sender or the message, or the noise. The answer is the receiver. It is important to understand as much as possible about the person with whom you are communicating. Therefore, if communication is not effective, whose fault is it? The answer is the sender. I know you are having trouble believing that you are responsible for ineffective communication. But to communicate effectively, you need to know your receiver. If the receiver speaks only Spanish and you send the message in English, you will not be effective. For those of you with siblings, do your parents discipline each child similarly? Of course not, because they know that each child responds differently to different types of punishments. Since you are the sender who wants the results, you have to encode the message in a way that the receiver can understand ideas. Remember that communication is not just talking and that action speaks louder than words. It takes work to communicate effectively.

Communication Context

Intrapersonal Communication

Intrapersonal communication is communication with yourself. Since the process of communication is transaction, you function as both the sender and receiver of the message. Unfortunately, sometimes we communicate ineffectively with ourselves. Too often we tell ourselves the wrong things. Dr. Shad Helmstetter (1987) in his book *What Do I*

Say When I Talk to Myself addresses the concerns when intrapersonal communication is ineffective. He provides short sentences that individuals can repeat daily to improve their self-image. He calls this *self-talk*. The premise behind self-talk is that everything we hear, see, and do is recorded in our brain through our five senses. Through the *law of repetition* the more you or others repeat messages, the more the messages are stored permanently in your brain. Whether good or bad, the more the messages are repeated to you, or you repeat them, the more it becomes who you are. Positive messages equal positive images and negative messages equate to negative images. Athletes will never say to themselves before a game: *I am going to lose. I am going to play badly. Or, I can't do this.* Similarly, you should never say before an exam: *I'm going to fail. I don't know the information.* Or, *I can't do this*. See how it works? Be careful what or who you listen to because they affect your subconscious and self-image.

Interpersonal Communication

Interpersonal communication is communication with other people. There are six major principles of interpersonal communication. We cannot not communicate! This statement means you are always communicating. This is one of the most debated principles because some scholars believe there must be intentionality to communicate while others say it does not matter.

Communication is irreversible. Once you send the message, you cannot take it back. So if you and your partner had a disagreement and you text that *I am breaking up with you. It is OVER*, you cannot take that message back. You can explain why you send it. But once the message is sent you cannot reverse it.

Communication involves ethical choices. As a communicator, we have the moral choice not to say things that will hurt, mislead, or affect lives in a negative way. My one-year-old started saying, "You look funny" when she meant "That was funny." I had to explain to her that it is not nice to say someone looks funny because it could hurt that person's feelings.

The meaning is in the individual. We addressed this earlier when we examined the five factors for determining meaning.

Interpersonal communication is how we build and maintain relationships with others.

Interpersonal communication effectiveness can be learned. Since it is a skill, we can learn to communicate more effectively.

Brian Tracy, the author of the *Eat Your Frog* books, provides us with *Three Ways to Improve Your Communication Skills* on his YouTube Success Channel. He offers the following advice to become a better great conversationalist. First, pause three to five seconds before replying to someone to avoid interrupting. This is done to show the other person that you are listening, and to hear the person better. Secondly, do not assume that you understand what someone is saying. If you are unsure, ask the question: "How do you mean?" The question forces the person to elaborate. Thirdly, paraphrase the speaker's words in your words: "So what you are saying is ..." Or "What you asked me was ... ?" Paraphrasing shows you are trying to understand and that you are listening. Once people see that you are listening to them, they are more likely to trust you and connect with you because people like to feel that someone is hearing them.

Four Types of Interpersonal Communication

Dyadic communication is communication between two individuals. When you are on the phone speaking or texting with your friend in a one-on-one conversation, you're engaging in dyadic communication. If you are at a job interview, you're engaging in dyadic communication.

Small group communication is communication among three or more individuals interacting with each other to come up with a common goal. So when you're on your social media chat group or talking with three or more of your friends about which movie you should attend, you are engaging in small group communication.

Public communication is a speaker addressing an audience or group of people. The president delivering a speech to the American people is an example of public communication. You can deliver speeches to inspire, to inform, to entertain, to convince, or to persuade a small or a large audience.

Mass communication is when an organization communicates to a large group. Newspapers, magazines, billboards, radio, and television are all forms of mass communication. Dr. Michael Morgan, professor of communication at the University of Massachusetts, stated on eHow (2009) that a book was one of the first mass-produced products. Hundreds of prints of the same messages were distributed to thousands of people, which leads to the concept of *agenda setting*. Who sets the agenda for how you think? For most people, it is the media. The media use words, create images, and present views based on that organization's agenda. Some media stations are liberal in their views while others are conservative. So who decides what is newsworthy? Who sets the agenda for how you think or what you think?

Why Study Communication?

Why study communication? Why should I learn about communication? I communicate every day. I am a good communicator. Communication, however, is a skill. If you work on improving your skills, then you'll improve your ability to communicate effectively. As communication professors, our goal is to help you strengthen your communication skills through practice so you can become a more effective communicator. After assisting you in clearing up some basic misconceptions you might have about communication and developing your communication skills, you will improve your relationships with your friends, family, and coworkers. Professor James McCoy (2011) in his YouTube video *Why Study Communication?* states that researchers asked CEOs and human resource hiring managers of Fortune 500 companies what skills are most critical for helping college graduates gain and maintain employment. The top answers were oral communication, interpersonal skills, and listening skills. Your ability to get along with your coworkers is vital. When asked what skills are needed to be a good manager or leader, the answers were strong oral and written communication skills, the ability to listen, and the ability to have good relationships with coworkers.

Thus, communication is a process in which you share and understand ideas. Our goal is to develop our skills to become more effective communicators, to build and strengthen relationships with our friends and family, and to influence other people's lives.

Credit

- Fig. 1.2: Copyright © Viniciuslima94 (CC BY-SA 4.0) at https://commons.wikimedia.org/wiki/File:Fig7_tipaper.png.

CHAPTER 2

Getting Started

What is Public Speaking?

Public speaking is an individual addressing a group of people. The Chapman University Survey on American Fears (2014) found that the number one fear in the United States is public speaking while the number four fear is death by drowning, meaning that most people are more afraid of giving the eulogy than being in the coffin. Fear of public speaking is a real fear that you may have, but some people say that an acronym for fear is false evidence appearing real. It is a real emotion that is all in the mind. It is not happening now but it is a fear of something happening in the future. But if you take the time to organize your presentation, you can reduce your fear.

Before you put together your presentation, there are six preparatory steps:

Step 1: Selecting your topic

Step 2: Narrowing your topic

Step 3: Determining your purpose

Step 4: Developing your central idea

Step 5: Developing main ideas

Step 6: Researching your topic

Step 1: Selecting Your Topic

Selection of the Topic

Before you choose your topic, you should know your topic is suitable for your audience, the occasion, and yourself.

The Audience

To make your presentation more effective, you must know your audience. Who is the intended audience? Why are they there to listen to you? Every presentation has an intended audience. Commercials, television shows, video games, etc., all have intended audiences. Therefore, before constructing, writing, and delivering your speech, you too must perform an audience analysis. Without knowing this information, your chance of delivering a successful presentation is very slim. An audience analysis is the process of gathering information about your audience to make sure the information you provide them is at the appropriate level. Audience analysis will ensure your presentation is audience-centered and not speaker-centered. Remember, your receiver is the most important element in the communication process. You cannot leave it to chance that your audience will understand, relate to, or appreciate your message. It is your responsibility to know your audience. When you know the characteristics and beliefs of your audience, you will become a more effective communicator.

It is important to learn the psychographics and demographics of your audience. Psychographics are the common beliefs, values, and lifestyles of your audience while the demographics are the common traits your audience possesses. Ask yourself the question: What are some commonalities among your audience? Let's examine some of the general commonalities between you and your audience. I am sure you can think of others.

Age: It is important to know the age level of the audience. Certain age groups are interested in certain topics. For example, what might be necessary information for a 45-year-old might be boring and not relevant to a 15-year-old.

Culture: Culture dictates our beliefs system. What might be relevant to one culture might be viewed entirely different by another. Some cultures might bury someone who dies in the morning before sundown, while other cultures might take days, weeks, or even years before the individual gets a proper burial. As a speaker, you must understand that people's cultural norms are important to them. Therefore, it is important that you understand your audience's cultural norms so that you do not insult or offend that audience.

Gender: In general, it is often said that men and women speak different languages and view life differently because of cultural norms and beliefs. Boys are usually taught to be tough and not to show emotions while girls are taught to be feminine and polite. Today these values are changing; however, they still exist in some cultures.

Education level: Education does not only refer to formal academic training. It also relates to the degree of knowledge your audience knows about your topic. Knowing this will help you determine their level of interest in the topic. It is important to present new, current, and correct information in your speech. You want your presentation to be timely and interesting.

The Occasion

The physical setting: Physical setting of the speaking venue should never be a surprise. Always take the time to know the number of people attending, the place, and any other physical attributes of the speaking situation to make sure your topic is appropriate.

Knowing how many people will be in attendance will help you prepare properly for the day of your presentation. You can determine if you need any special equipment such as a microphone or PowerPoint, etc. The larger the audience, the more difficult it will be for them to see and hear you. Also, prepare enough handouts for everyone. Always make sure you have enough handouts for every member of your audience and if you do not have enough, take members' names and make sure you forward them the information. Getting the information to the audience promptly will ensure that it thinks favorably of you and your message.

The venue: How will the site look? Are you inside or outside? Is it a church, school, or banquet setting? This is important information to know. Why? It speaks to the level of distraction that your audience will face. Although I graduated some 20 years ago with my Doctorate degree, I can still remember the plane that was skywriting while the guest speaker was talking. I cannot remember the speech or the topic or the message, but I do remember the plane writing, "Will you marry me … ?" And the applause and cheers for the young lady who received the proposal. Our graduation was outside, and the speaker was under a canopy. The speaker had no idea the applause was not for her. If you are delivering a speech in this setting, the level of communication noise will be greater than it would be than if you were inside. How about giving a speech in a ballpark with the audience surrounding you? How would you adjust as you speak? Your goal is to connect with your audience, so you must turn your body so that everyone feels included.

Here are some common questions you should ask about the occasion.

The Purpose

1. What is the reason for the gathering?
2. What type of event is it?
3. What will occur before or after I present?
4. Is there something occurring that might add or take away from the effectiveness of your topic?
5. Are there other speakers?
6. What is the size of the audience?
7. Why did you choose me?
8. What are your and the audience's expectations for me?
9. Will the audience be allowed to participate by asking questions?

The Place

1. How large is the room?
2. What is the location: indoor or outdoor?
3. What is the shape of the room? (i.e., circular, U-shape, etc.)
4. What type of room? (i.e., classroom, banquet hall, auditorium, etc.)
5. What facilities are available? (i.e., lectern, stage, type of microphones, computer, projector, etc.)
6. What is the address or location?

The Time

1. What is the date of your presentation?
2. Will it be in the morning, afternoon, evening, or nighttime?
3. The length for your presentation
4. The position of your presentation in the program etc.

You can get the information you need by asking the host questions, surveying the audience, conducting research on the Internet, or by physically going to the venue.

Yourself

Not only is it important to understand your audience and the occasion, but you also need to know yourself, and your level of commitment to the topic.

You should ask yourself the following questions when picking a topic:

- How passionate are you about this subject?
- Do you care about the issue? If you do not, your lack of commitment will show in your delivery. Choose something that you feel strongly about. Do not pick a topic to impress your audience or your professor.
- How much do you know about the topic? If you do not know a lot about the topic, are you willing to do the research?
- How comfortable are you with the topic?
- How much time do you have to invest or research?
- Do you know more about the topic than your audience?

These are important questions for you to answer because they will help you in picking a topic that will benefit both the audience and you. If you are connected and passionate about the topic, it will show in your delivery and you will be able to transfer that passion to the audience. There are two basic methods to find a topic: You can either brainstorm or do research. Regardless of the method, your topic must be audience-centered.

Step 2: Narrowing Your Topic

Narrowing the Topic

Once you have done your initial research, you can choose and narrow your topic. Remember, your goal is to narrow the topic so that it fits the audience, the required time limitations, and the purpose. One way to do this is to have as many variables as possible in your thesis. You can do this by breaking the topic down into subcategories. For instance, let us say you have to deliver an informative speech of six to eight minutes. Your topic is music. Can you give an effective six- to eight-minute speech with the thesis: "Today I am going to inform you about music"? This would be impossible because music is such a huge category. There is no way you could do an effective presentation on the topic of music alone because there is too much information on the subject. So add another variable to the topic. You might pick a genre of music. If I choose soca music, I now have two variables (soca and music). Can I deliver an effective speech on soca music? Again, the topic is too big; soca music has been around for decades. So add another variable and break it down further to include the history of soca music. Again, ask yourself this question: Can I effectively deliver a six- to eight-minute information presentation on the history of soca music? As long as the topic is bigger than the time limitation, the answer will be "no."

Once you narrow the topic, the thesis can be "Today I will inform you about the history of soca music from the Republic of Trinidad and Tobago (T&T) during the early '50s." How many variables are there? The answer is five (history, soca, music, T&T, the early '50s). Keep in mind the more variables, the stronger the focus and organization. Make sure you do not overly narrow the topic because you will not be able to find the research information. If you find yourself in that predicament, just change or remove one of the variables to open up the topic.

Step 3: Determining the Purposes

There are five primary purposes of a speech: to inform, to entertain, to inspire, to convince, and to persuade. Let us define each one.

If your goal of the speech is to inform, you are increasing the audience's knowledge about the topic by providing them with new information. *If you tell the audience what it already knows, you will fail to achieve the goal.*

If the goal of your speech is to entertain, you are providing enjoyment for your audience. So the speech will include satire, and the topic will be light and amusing.

If the goal of your speech is to inspire, you will strengthen attitudes, opinions, and beliefs already held by the audience. You are motivating the audience similar to a preacher or motivational speaker.

If the goal of your speech is to convince, you are changing the attitudes, opinions, and beliefs of the audience.

If the goal of your speech is to persuade, you are changing the attitudes, opinions, and beliefs in order to change their actions. To persuade you must first convince but your primary goal is to change behavior. Therefore, you must tell the audience what actions it should or should not do. For instance, I can convince you that smoking is bad, but I have to persuade you to stop smoking.

Step 4: Determine the Central Idea

The central idea is the behavioral objective that you want the audience to do. Ask yourself the following question:

By the end of my speech, what do I want the audience to be able to do?

Answers:

- By the end of my speech, the audience will be able to stop texting while driving.
- By the end of my speech, the audience will be able to bake a carrot cake.
- By the end of my speech, the audience will be able to tell others about the attacks on the World Trade Center.

This question will further help you generate the thesis sentence. The statements must be in a complete declarative sentence with a single central idea. The language must be direct and specific.

Step 5: Generating Main Ideas

Once you have your thesis, it should be straightforward to decide your main ideas. Just look at the 5 Ws and 1 H: WHO? WHAT? WHERE? WHEN? WHY? HOW? For instance:

- Who are people texting while driving?
- What are the causes why people are texting while driving?
- When are people texting while driving?
- Why are people texting while driving?
- How are people texting while driving?

Pick the best three (3) areas for your main ideas.

Step 6: Researching Your Topic

When researching your presentation, always critically evaluate your information.

Your information should be current, logical, and objective. Always integrate the research into your speech to avoid plagiarizing someone else's work. Plagiarizing is taking someone else's work and ideas and passing it off as your own. Always give credit to the source of your information. In higher levels of learning, it is all about how you know what you know.

So how do you know what you know? You can know due to personal knowledge, experience, observation, primary research, and secondary research.

Primary research is your surveys and interviews. Secondary research comes from books, articles, newspapers, statistical sources, biographical references, government documents, and electronic-based resources. Do not use Wikipedia. Use refereed journals and databases for your research. These databases can be accessed for free through your school's library. If you do not know how to use them, ask your school librarian for assistance.

CHAPTER 3

Organizing Your Presentation

It is important that you organize your presentation in an easy-to-follow format. A properly organized presentation makes it easier for the audience to understand the information and to connect with the topic and presenter. Your presentation must have a clearly organized introduction, body, and conclusion; regardless of the situation, you should always have these three elements. Even a 30-second commercial has an introduction, body, and conclusion. In your presentation, you must tell the audience what you want them to know (introduction), tell it to the audience (body), and then tell the audience what you just told them (conclusion). So let us start by examining the parts of the introduction.

The Introduction

The introduction is crucial because it is the first thing your audience will hear. It is the audience's first impression of you as a speaker. The old saying that *your first impression is a lasting impression* stands true here. If the introduction is not easy to follow, the audience will be turned off by your presentation. So what do you put into the introduction of your paper or speeches? The average introduction will only fulfill these three purposes. It will grab the attention of the audience, tell the purpose, and preview the main points in the body. When the other 2 purposes of the introduction are not added, the introduction will lie flat.

Your introduction must have five goals: the attention-getter (AG), the thesis statement (TS), the reason-to-listen statement (RS), the credibility statement (CS), and the preview statement (PS). You can fulfill these purposes with either a sentence or a couple of sentences. You can even use one sentence to accomplish a few goals. How you achieve these goals will be determined by the length of your presentation. Let us thoroughly examine each part and their purposes.

The Attention-Getter

The attention-getter is the first thing in your introduction. Its purpose is to grab the attention of the audience and keep it engaged. Why would someone want to listen to you speak? How can you get him or her interested in your topic? The answers to these questions will give you the purpose for your attention-getter. You should never start the speech with your name or the topic. It is the job of the master of ceremonies to introduce you and your topic. Always start with your attention-getter. Would you tell someone valuable information if he or she is not listening to you? So why would you present the relevant information of your topic if the audience is not listening to you?

There are many forms of the attention-getter. First is a *question*. There are two types of questions. The first is a survey question in which you ask the audience to provide a census. An example of a *survey question* is "How many of you smoke cigarettes? Please indicate by raising your hand." Once you have surveyed the audience, you have to provide the audience with the results. Therefore, your next sentence should go like this: "I see by the show of hands 50% of you smoke cigarettes." The survey question is not the best way to open your speech. Why? The main reason is that the audience might not want to participate. Therefore, your results will not support your topic. If only 20% of the audience smokes cigarettes, then can you make the next statement? "Today I am going to talk about the harms of smoking cigarettes." No, because the audience will be thinking why are you talking to us if we don't smoke. You have just increased, NOT minimized, the *noise* in the *Communication Process*. If you choose to survey your audience, it is best to do so before the speech. Surveying the audience before the speech would be a part of your audience analysis. Once you receive the answers, you can tailor the speech to the audience.

The better type of question to open your address is the *rhetorical question*. The rhetorical question is a question that you do not want the audience to answer physically. It does, however, stimulate their minds to think of the answer. You should place rhetorical questions throughout your speech to keep the audience's attention and to engage it.

Examples of how to start a rhetorical question:

- What do you think of when you hear the words ... ?
- Do you know that ... ?
- What would you do if ... ever happened to you?
- What would you do if you were faced with ... ?
- Imagine if ... happened. How would you handle it?

Quotations or dramatic statements are another method of attention-getters. When you provide a quotation, you must always provide the reference information. But starting a presentation with the words "according to" will not grab your audience's attention about your topic. Most people will instead think this will be a boring presentation. Instead, place the reference information and date after the quotation. For instance, don't state, "According to Dr. Martin Luther King Jr., in his speech *I have a Dream*, he stated, 'I have a dream.'" Instead, it would be more interesting if you said, "'I have a dream'—these words spoken by Dr. Martin Luther King Jr. in ..." You can only do this effectively in the attention-getter. When stating quotations within the speech, always prepare the audience to listen intelligently by presenting the reference information first. The same holds true for *startling facts or statistics*, the third type of AG.

You can open your presentation with *startling facts or statistics*. For instance, you can state, "In 2010, 1,000 people died. In 2013, 20,000 died. It is estimated that in 2016, 100,000 people will be dead. These statistics taken from ..." Startling facts or statistics lets your listener know how significant or large the problem or topic is. Other types of visual aids that sometimes need references would be *visual or audio aids* if taken from someone else. Sometimes you can start a presentation by showing illustrations, short videos, or objects. Again, for greater effect, show the aids before giving the references. One of the best uses of visual aid that I have seen to open a speech was at a graduation when the valedictorian started her presentation by taking pictures of the crowd for about 30 seconds. Everyone was wondering what she was doing. She then proceeded to say: "Images, for the last 4 years we have collected many images, and today, I will capture my last." The crowd erupted in applause. That theme was woven throughout the speech, as she presented many special events during the last four years.

So if you are the type of person who is *humorous*, you can start your presentation with *humor*. But humor is not just telling jokes. It is not a one-man comedy show. You must relate your jokes to your topic or the occasion. Humor helps to connect you with your audience and to make the audience like you. If you can place it throughout your presentation, the audience will find you likable. Everyone wants to have a good time; however, it can be tricky to open your presentation with humor if you are not a funny person. The good thing about humor is that if people don't laugh, then they did not know it was meant to be humorous so just keep talking.

You can start your presentation with a *reference to historical events, recent developments, or the previous speeches*. Once again, all must relate to your topic. When you use events that are fresh in the audience's mind, it is then easier to persuade or affect the audience because it can relate to the information. For instance, if you hear something recent in the news and it relates to your topic, you can start the speech referring to the event. This shows your audience that you are on top of things and current in your information. You can only use references to a preceding speech if another speaker said something profound in his or her address and it relates to the topic. Therefore, you are adjusting your speech on the spot, which provides added value for using the extemporaneous style of delivery. We will examine this more in Chapter 4. Nevertheless, always have a prepared written attention-getter.

Personal references can add value to your credibility. This indicates to your audience that you are personally attached to the topic. If, for example, you are a recovering alcoholic who killed someone while under the influence of alcohol, you can use your story to start a speech persuading the audience against drinking and driving. Remember, you have an ethical responsibility to your audience members not to mislead them. Do not make up a *short story* to get the audience's sympathy. No one wants to think he or she was manipulated by you. You can start the speech with a fictional story if you alert the audience that it is fictional. You should start by saying, "Imagine that ..." Or, "Imagine if this happens ..."

These are a few types of attention-getters that you can use to open your presentation. You might be able to think of others, but whatever type you choose, there are a few rules that you should follow. First, the attention-getter is the first thing in your introduction. Don't start the speech with your name or the topic. Second, the attention-getter must relate to your topic. Third, it should not be offensive to the audience or scare the audience so much that it cannot focus on your presentation. For instance, if your speech is about gun control, you should not bring a semiautomatic Uzi and point it at the audience, and then place it on a desk facing the audience. The communication noise will be too much for an audience that is not accustomed to guns. Their focus will be on the weapon. They will wonder if it is real or loaded, and thus will not be able to concentrate on the speech. Likewise, be careful about images you show the audience. If the picture is too shocking, you might not be able to get the audience to focus on your speech. Finally, you should make the attention-getter interesting for your audience. Therefore, it is important that you conduct your audience analysis. You can use a few different attention getters to open your presentation.

Thesis Statement

From your general and specific purposes, you will be able to formulate your thesis. The *thesis statement* is the main idea you wish to convey to the audience. It states the purpose of your speech in a declarative sentence. The thesis should be clear and simply stated. You can use such wording as:

- Today I want to inform you ...
- My purpose here is to inform you ...
- It is important to understand ...

Never state in your thesis that you are going to persuade or to convince. These are words that place the audience on the defensive. If the speaker says, "Today I am going to persuade you that you must eat healthy," your initial response will be *No, you are not*. As stated previously, people don't like to think that others are manipulating them. For persuasive speech, it is best to write the thesis in the form of a problem. Thus, you can state, *today we will discuss the harms of eating unhealthy or the major problems that can occur when people do not eat healthy*. You will only have one thesis.

Reason-to-Listen Statement

The *reason-to-listen statement* is paramount because it is the statement that connects the speaker, the topic, and the audience. It tells the audience why your topic is important. What is the benefit of your topic to the audience? Why should it listen to you? What value your speech will have for the audience? To write this statement, you need to understand your audience's wants, needs, desires, and fears.

What motivates your audience and why? There are some general things that people want. They are life, happiness, peace of mind, love, wealth, etc. You must, however, write the statement for your intended audience. I cannot emphasize enough that you must know your audience if you want to be an effective communicator. So write and then rewrite and then rewrite your reason-to-listen statement so that it impacts your audience. This goal must be woven throughout your entire introduction by using descriptive words.

Credibility Statement

The *credibility statement* shows your audience that you are knowledgeable about your topic. It tells the audience why they should believe or trust you. There are two methods to establish your credibility. One method is by stating your credentials. For instance, if you are a doctor and have been working on AIDS research, you can say, *as a physician who has been working on AIDS research for the past 10 years, I am here to discuss my findings*. The audience will be more willing to accept the information you are presenting because they see you as credible. So tell the audience how you know what you know. What is your background, education, or experiences as they relate to the topic? Choose your credentials as they relate to your topic. You will not discuss your matchbook collection hobby for a topic dealing with baking cakes.

Another method to establish your credibility is to link your credibility to an expert by stating a credible reference. Stating a credible reference shows the audience you have done research, and experts in the supports your views. You can present the references by saying, *According to (name, credentials) in the (reference) on (date) it states* ... Some other words to introduce references are: *1) ... explains in; 2) ... says in; 3) as reported by ... 4) ... writes that.*

Be specific when writing your credibility statement. You should never state *research shows that* because this statement is too general and ambiguous. It will cause the audience to doubt and question the information you are presenting. Tell the audience the name of the studies and who conducted it.

Having a strong credibility statement will build the audience's confidence in your topic and you. It helps to build and maintain your ethos. The Greek philosopher Aristotle established three types of appeals that a speaker can use when organizing a speech. They are logos, ethos, and pathos. *Logos* is your logical appeals: your facts, proofs, structure of arguments, statistics, etc. *Pathos* is your emotional appeals. *Ethos* is your ethical appeals: the speaker's character, intelligence, and goodwill toward the audience. Ethos is in the mind of the audience and is easily broken if you lose trust with the audience. Once ethos is lost, it's hard for the speaker to re-establish it. So make sure you check your facts and references to ensure they are correct before presenting it to your audience. You can have a few credibility statements in the introduction.

Preview Statement

The *preview statement* prepares the audience to listen intelligently to your topic. It states the areas you will address in the body of the speech. It gives the audience the road map of your speech. It is your navigator system. To generate your preview statement, use the 5 W's and one H: who, what, where, when, why, and how. Do not overly explain the information. The explanation belongs in the body of the speech. The preview statement is a tease. You are wetting the audience's appetite for what is to come. When you elaborate too much, you ruin the anticipation for the audience and you lose its interest. A sample template:

Today we will examine (first point in the body), then we will look at (second point in the body), and finally we will address (third point in the body).

Once you learn how to generate the preview sentence, then you can become more creative with your sentence. But don't be too creative. Remember that simple is better. If you create too much you can lose your audience. Your goal is not to hide the information from your audience but to set it up so that the audience can easily follow your presentation. Nothing frustrates an audience more than not knowing what you are saying. You will only have one preview statement.

Guidelines for the Introduction

Like the attention-getter, there are guidelines to follow to help you generate a solid introduction. First, when structuring your introduction, the attention-getter is first, and the preview statement is last. Think of them as the bread of a turkey sandwich. We all make a sandwich differently. Some people like to place the mayo on the bread. Others will put the mayo on the turkey. But regardless of where you put the condiments, the slices of bread, in most instances, will go on the outside.

Second, do not start your speech with your name or the topic. Starting the speech with your name and the topic is like beginning the speech with your credibility and thesis statements. Remember, you should always get the attention of the audience first. Then you can acknowledge the important individuals in the audience.

Third, be brief and to the point. Every sentence in your introduction should meet one of the five purposes. Do not add information such as history or definitions because they belong in the body of the speech.

Fourth, do not apologize for mistakes that you might make or have made. For instance, don't apologize to the audience for the following: 1) forgetting something, 2) being nervous, 3) being a novice speaker, and 4) taking too much of its time, etc. Why? It will decrease your credibility and introduce internal communication noise in the mind of your audience. Plus, the audience does not care. They want you to perform and to perform to the best of your ability.

Fifth, do not refer to time. Time is relative. What might be short to one person is long to another. When the speaker refers to time, again internal communication noise will increase in the audience's mind. Have you ever been at a graduation and the speaker said, *I am not going to take up too much of your time I know you want to celebrate?* After the speaker makes that statement, within three minutes you begin to think the speech is too long and start questioning when it will end. The audience can no longer concentrate on your message. Do NOT use phrases such as these that refer to time:

- I will be short.
- I will not take too much of your time.
- I will only be a few minutes.
- I don't have much time with you today.

Sixth, do not insult or offend your audience. As a speaker, you don't want to seem conceited or condescending toward your audience. Do not use words the audience cannot understand. There are five types of people in any audience:

The friendly audience that supports your message. These people support your message and what you have to say.

The hostile audience is against your message and does not want to listen to what you have to say. Depending upon the level of hostility, the audience might even try to prevent you from speaking through booing or throwing things at you. Therefore, you don't want to turn your friendly audience into a hostile audience by insulting or offending them.

The critical audience is better known as a thinking audience. Critical not in a negative sense but in a positive sense. These are the people who will listen with an open mind. They will weigh the evidence before making a decision. They ask questions and seek further research before making a decision. Therefore, you must provide credible research and logically structured arguments.

The apathetic audience just doesn't care about your message. Some call this a captured audience; they have to be there but don't care about your message. You need to have a strong reason-to-listen statement for this type of audience.

You will always have a mixture of all four in your audience. Depending on the occasion, you will have a higher percentage of one type of people in your audience. Write the speech for a *critical audience* but delivery it as if you were delivering it to a *friendly audience*. This strategy will reduce your anxiety and ensure your speech is properly written.

Body

The body of the speech is where you develop your main ideas. It should be well organized and clearly written. You should follow the KISS rule—Keep It Short and Sweet. You want to have three (3) clear, main points regardless of the time length. You might be able to have a fourth but no more than four (4). It is, however, best to use three main points when developing the body of your speech. When you have too many points, your audience will not retain the information. Instead of having 15 points, have three main points and develop those points well. To generate your main points, use who, who, where, when, and how. When selecting the points, choose points that are relevant to your audience and phrase them in a parallel style. Also, you should develop distinct, balanced main points. Each main point should be about the same time length. Make sure your arguments are cohesive and organized in a logical sequence.

Organizational Patterns

There are five basic organization patterns that you can use for the body of your speech. **Temporal organizational pattern** is organizing the body of the text based on a time sequence. For example, if you are writing about fashion in the United States, you can talk about fashion in the '60s, '80s, or '90s. You could also use a chronological sequence: past, present, and future. The order would be from greater to lesser, or lesser to greater. **Spatial organizational pattern** is organizing the body of the text based on space or geography. For example, if you are speaking of fashion in the United States, you can talk about fashion in the North, the South, or the central United States. The **topical organizational pattern** is organizing the body of the text based on subtopics that are strongly linked. Most students do not use the topical organizational pattern well because the link is not very strong. For example, if you are speaking of fashion in the United States and address the clothes, the designer, and the runway, the link is not very strong. You can easily go on tangents because your focus is not narrowed. You can fix this by adding one or two other factors. For instance, your focus will be stronger if you address the problems that are occurring in fashion in the United States and address the problems with the clothes, the problems with the designers, and the problems with the runway. **Problem-solution organizational pattern** is organizing the body of the text based on outlining the problem and then addressing the solution of a problem. You should use this organizational pattern for persuasive appeals. **Cause to effect/effect to** cause organizational pattern addresses the reasons for a problem and then examines the effects. You can combine it with the problem-solution organization pattern to develop a strong persuasive speech.

Oral vs. Written Style

There is a difference between the way we write and the way we speak. When choosing words, you should choose words that are specific, concrete words. Choose words that are simple. You should not sound as if you swallowed a dictionary. A speech that is laden with definitions lies flat. The audience will not be able to understand your message.

Oral Style of Communication	Written Style of Communication
Uses more short phrases and fragments	Uses compound, complex sentences
Uses a lot of Repetition	Uses less variations
Uses more informal language	Uses more formal language
Uses more words with fewer syllables	Uses Lengthy words
More personal	More formal

Transitions

The transition is a bridge from one point to another. Use transitions between the main points in the body of your text to make your points cohesive. Use a transition from the first main point to the second main point, and form the second main point to the third main point. An example of a transition is *now that we have discussed ... Let us discuss ...* You have to tell the audience where you are coming from and where you are going. Once you get good at writing transitions, you can write large papers. Most students get upset when their professor assigns a 30-page paper. If you understand how to write transitions, the task becomes easy. Can you write a three-page paper? If yes, then you can write a 30-page paper. It is a matter of perceptive. A 30-page paper is three (3) 10-page papers with an introduction and conclusion and linked together with transitions. A 10-page paper is three (3) three-page papers with an introduction and conclusion and linked together with transitions. Yes, you got it. A three-page paper is a bunch of paragraphs linked together with transitions.

Some ways to make your speech cohesive are using figures of speech (words or phrases that have meaning other than their literal meaning) and transitions, such as:

1. Sign Posts: using numbers or letters to organize your points. Be careful that you keep track of your numbers
2. Internal Previews: presenting how you will handle the topic
3. Internal Summary: restating your points
4. Metaphors: comparing two unlike ideas or things (i.e., time is money)
5. Simile: comparing two unlike things, using like or as (i.e., blind as a bat)
6. Alliteration: repeating the beginning sounds of words in a phrase (i.e., she sells seashells)
7. Hyperbole: exaggerating for emphasis (i.e., "Everybody knows that ..." or "Big as a house")

8. Anaphora: using several phrases that begin with the same words (i.e., Julius Caesar's "I came, I saw, I conquered!")
9. Euphemism: using milder, more indirect words (i.e., pass away vs. die)
10. Interjection: words that stimulate emotions (i.e., Now, yes, wow). Be careful not to choose inappropriate ones like profanities or vocal fillers (i.e., um, huh, ok).
11. Acronyms: abbreviations created from the first letter of words (i.e., FBI or ATM)
12. Vivid examples
13. Rhetorical Questions: questions that do not need an answer
14. Analogy: comparing two similar things

Whatever you choose should be appropriate and simple enough for the audience to follow. Use figures of speech to make your speech come alive, so the audience can picture and relate to your topic.

Critical Thinking

Critical thinking is essential to effective communication. It aids us in structuring clear messages. We sometimes make errors or have fallacies in our critical thinking. We will take a look at it here:

Facts Versus Opinion

Sometimes people substitute opinions with facts, and because they speak with conviction, we tend to believe them. Facts are statements that can be proven to be true (example: 1 + 2 = 3). On the other hand, opinions are judgments, interpretation, predictions, or preferences (example: *The Black Panther* was an awesome movie). Opinions cannot be proven; however, they can be supported by arguable propositions. When you write your speech, use facts and arguable propositions to support your opinions. There are two forms of reasoning through opinions: inductive reasoning and deductive reasoning.

Inductive Reasoning Versus Deductive Reasoning

Inductive reasoning is when you reason from a specific point to a general point (example: A + B =AB, or Jane is in great shape, and she does exercise. Bill looks great and he does exercise. Kim has great muscle definition and she does swimming. Therefore, people who do exercise will look great.) You can use past facts to form new facts and conclusions. But be careful not to make hasty generalizations. A hasty generalization is when you make a generalization of a large population based on evidence from a smaller population (example: When Jane studies she gets an A on her exam. If everyone studies like Jane, they will get an A on the exam.) When generalizing, use words like some, many, most, or probably. Avoid using the words all, total, complete, always, never, and none. They suggest that there are no exceptions and will make the audience question your argument and information.

Deductive reasoning is going from general assumptions to specific assumptions (example: The mailman does not deliver the mail on legal holidays. Today is a legal holiday. No mail will be delivered today.) Deductive reasoning is expressed in three parts, called syllogism. There is a major premise, a minor premise, and a conclusion. For example:

Major Premise: Members of the marching band take music classes.
Minor Premise: John is a member of the marching band.
Conclusion: John takes music classes.

If the premises are true, the conclusion will be true. Sometimes the conclusion can be false, as in this example:

Major Premise: All members of the marching band are in music class.
Minor Premise: John is in music class.
Conclusion: John is a member of the marching band.

The syllogism is valid if the reasoning is logical. Here are some basic fallacies in reasoning that speakers use: *ad hominem arguments* attack the person rather than the issue (i.e., Senator John missed every important vote this session. He is untrustworthy.); *either or/if then* arguments assume there are only two sides of an argument with no alternative point of view (i.e., 1. Either we vote for him, or we will have big problems. 2. If we don't vote for him, then life as we know it will not be the same.); *non sequiturs* do not follow deductive reasoning (i.e., My sister recommended this book, so it has to be good.); while *false analogies* compare two things that are like or not alike in some way; *begging the question* builds the arguments on unproven assumptions or opinions (i.e., Fireworks are illegal because they are not good.); a *bandwagon argument* is that we should accept or reject because everyone or the right people are doing it (i.e., All doctors agree ...). As a speaker you have to be able to structure you arguments correctly because you have several ethical responsibilities to your audience:

1. You should tell the truth—present credible facts to support your claims.
2. You should know your topic well—examine both sides of your issue, and test your sources.
3. You should accept responsibility for what your say—don't use propaganda or plagiarism.
4. You should listen critically to the other side and not stop them from presenting.

The Conclusion

The conclusion is your last chance to make an impact and to drive your point home. It is the last thing the audience will hear. And remember that based on the Primary (Bieri, 1955) many people remember more the last thing they heard. The conclusion has three parts: the summary statement, the reinforcement statement, and the closing statement. It is easy to write because it is a blueprint of your introduction. Your *summary statement* is equivalent to your *thesis* and *preview statements* but in past tense. Likewise, the *reinforcement statement* is equal to the *credibility and reason-to-listen statements*. The *closing statement* balanced out your *attention-getter*. Let us examine each statement in detail:

Summary Statement (S/S)

The summary statement's purpose is to remind the audience of your major areas. It states your thesis and three main points. It is, however, in past tenses. For example: *Today we discussed the dangerous consequences of people smoking in cars with toddlers by examining the cause, the major effects, and some solutions to solve this terrible problem.*

Reinforcement Statement (R/S)

The reinforcement or re-emphasis statement reminds the audience the importance of your topic. It is equivalent to the reason-to-listen statement in the introduction. The reinforcement or re-emphasis statement is the last chance you have to drive your premise home.

Closing Statement

The closing statement closes and is the last thing the audience will hear. It closes the speech with impact and refers to the attention-getter. It should end on an emotional high for the audience, and it must signal the end of your speech. The audience should not have to wonder if the speech is over. You can end with a rhetorical question, a plea for action, a story, or a dramatic statement. Whatever you use should build to the climax of your presentation. The audience should burst in applause.

Guidelines for the Conclusion

There are some important rules to consider when writing and delivering your conclusion. *First,* do not apologize for any mistakes you made in the speech. You should not remind your audience of your shortcomings because to do so will leave your audience with the impression that you are not credible. *Second,* the summary statement must be first, and the closing statement should be last. You must have a closing statement; do not leave your audience hanging. *Third,* only have one conclusion, which made sense when you wrote the conclusion. Of course, you wrote only one conclusion. But some novice speakers will conclude and then remember they had forgotten something, then start to inform the audience of the forgotten information. Now they will try to end again. It is better to leave the information out and readdress it in the question-and-answer session or at another time. *Fourth,* do not introduce new information in the conclusion. All new information should be developed in the body of the speech. The purpose of the conclusion is to summarize, reinforce, and close. *Fifth,* do not say, "In conclusion," "I am going to conclude," "I am going to stop any minute again." Why? These are buzzwords that prevent the audience from listening to your speech. It is the same principle as when your professor says, "Tomorrow you will be doing ...". What do you then start doing? You start to pack up and half of the information your professor says after that statement you do not hear. If the professor announces a quiz or homework, half the class will not get the message. Again, you are referring to time. *Sixth,* do not drag the conclusion on and on. If you do not stop on time, the audience will be upset and you will lose the impact of your message. *Finally,* do not say, "*That's it*" or "*I am done*" or "*It is over.*" These statements are made because the speaker did not build the conclusion to a climax with words and delivery. The audience is left to guess whether the speech is over. The audience is looking at the speaker and the speaker is watching the audience. Therefore, the easiest phase to use is simply *"That's it"* to signal to the audience the speech is finished. "That's it," however, should never be a closing statement. Some people say you can utter "thank you" while others believe you should not say this because it takes away from your credibility. It's your judgment call but always remember that "thank you" is not a closing statement—it is in response to your audience's applause. You have to get the audience applauding before thanking them.

Once you organize your speech properly, the audience will be able to follow your presentation easily, and the audience will praise you as an effective speaker. Now let us look at making you a dynamic speaker.

CHAPTER 4

Delivery and Common Mistakes

So you have created the perfect presentation and now it is time to practice your delivery. You can have the best-written speech but if your delivery is not done correctly, your message will not be communicated effectively. Remember that in Chapter 1 you learn that 85%–90% of your communication comes from nonverbal and non-vocal communication. So, let us get you prepared to deliver a dynamic presentation.

Methods of Delivery

The delivery methods are the way the speech is presented to the audience. There are four basic methods of delivering your presentation: manuscript, memory, impromptu, and extemporaneous. Let us look more in-depth at each method by examining the advantages, the disadvantages, and the recommendations for using the methods correctly.

Manuscript

A manuscript speech is one delivered through a word-for-word text. Similar to the manuscript of a play, everything you are going to say will be written out. Manuscripts are good to use when you have a precise time limit. The news is very much scripted because they allot time for commercials. Media airtime is very expensive so if you buy airtime, whether on television or radio, you need to use the time wisely. So if you choose to use a manuscript as your method of delivery, what are the advantages?

Advantages

You will always know what to say. It will appear more polished because you will not stumble over your words or be lost for words. Everything is written out for you so you will not get lost. You will not go on tangents. Many speakers when freely speaking will tend to go off on tangents. They stray from their topic and speak on things unrelated. The speech will be well organized with a clear introduction, body, and conclusion. In addition, it will be well researched with current information. Most importantly, you have a written record of the speech. So you will be able to reproduce the speech over and over again. Although the advantages are great, there are many disadvantages to using the manuscript method of delivery.

Disadvantages

If you lose the script, there goes the speech. Speakers are known to leave the manuscript in the taxi or the hotel room. A manuscript restricts your movements. You are trapped behind a podium that creates a barrier between you and your audience. Whenever delivering a speech, it is best to remove all barriers between you and your audience. So get rid of the podium.

People tend to read the manuscript, which limits eye contact with the audience. The eyes are the mirrors to the soul. You have to look at your audience to engage them and establish a relationship. Without establishing a relationship with the audience, it is difficult to get your message across.

People tend to read in a monotone or mechanical manner. Some people are very poor readers and, as such, you do not want to listen to them read because they read in a monotone without any vocal variety, stumbling over their words. They may read too slow or too fast. Therefore, using a manuscript diminishes the speaker's ethos in the eyes of the audience. The speaker loses the focus of the audience and this creates more communication noise in the communication setting.

The manuscript can become a distraction for the audience. Once, during a conference, the speaker had the speech on a glass podium and proceeded to read the entire speech without making eye contact with the audience. While reading she would place the page to the right after she finished. After a while, the pages became a distraction because we kept waiting for the last page to be moved to the right. But most importantly, you cannot adjust the speech on the spot to match the responses of the audience.

Recommendations

If you are going to use a manuscript to deliver your speech, do not make the mistake and think that you do not have to practice the speech. On the contrary, you have to practice the speech so it appears you are not reading from a text. Ninety percent of your eye contact needs to be directed toward the audience. Just as with a news spokesperson, the manuscript should not be the central focus. Know your manuscript well. Watch congressional leaders, U.S. presidents, and news spokespersons to see how they use manuscripts.

Use a manuscript when you do not want to be misunderstood or you have a strict time limit. Write the speech in the oral style and practice it out loud with appropriate facial expressions, eye contact, vocal variety, gestures, and movements. Time the presentation a couple of times to make sure it the right length. Prepare the manuscript so it can be easily read. Use a large font size, triple spacing, and delivery clues, such as pause, slow down, speak up etc. Highlight areas that you have difficulty remembering or seeing. But most importantly, check that you have the manuscript before you leave the house, before you leave the taxi, and before you enter the speaking area.

Memory

When you deliver a speech from memory, the information is placed in your brain. Thus, you memorized your manuscript. This method can make you seems more credible because you appear to know your information.

Advantages

You have the same advantages provided by the manuscript speech because you will not memorize junk. So your speech will be well organized and researched.

You will have more eye contact because you have nothing to read from. Therefore, you will tend to focus more on the audience than the speech.

You are free to move around. With everything in your brain, there is no need to stand at a podium. You are free to move toward and away from the audience.

Your speech tends to be less monotone because you are focusing more on the audience than on the speech. The audience will believe that you are more knowledgeable. Use memory for short presentations when you want to look sincere and spontaneous.

Disadvantages

There are time requirements. Some people have excellent memories and can easily memorize documents. But for most people, this is not the case. It takes a while for the average person to memorize a 15- to 20-minute speech.

You can forget the information. If you forget the information there goes your speech. Under pressure, it becomes easy to forget your presentation. If you forget the information, the speech will be lost. Speakers tend to look at empty space, the ceiling, and the floor as if the words are written there. Speakers then sway from side to side as if swaying helps them remember.

You might tend to look unnatural because you speak to too quickly, too slowly, or very mechanically. Again this speech cannot be adapted to the responses of the audience.

If memory is your choice, here are some recommendations.

Recommendation

If you intend to use the memory method of delivery, you must know the speech so well that it flows fluently from your mouth. Have you ever listened to a speaker and you can see the speaker thinking? This is because the speaker is focusing on remembering the speech and not focusing on delivering the speech. What do I mean by this statement? Your ultimate goal is to connect with your audience. You have to speak to the audience, not at them. Have a conversation even if the speech is memorized. If you are delivering your speech and your brain tells you the next statement is wrong, press through because you are right—it is just your nerves playing tricks on you.

Impromptu

Impromptu is a speech delivery without any specific preparation. Have you ever been at a wedding, funeral, or award ceremony and been asked to speak? Well, that speech was an impromptu presentation. So, with so little or no preparation, is there anything positive that can be said for the impromptu presentation?

Advantages

It is passionate. Most people get caught up in the moment and speak from the heart in these situations. You have more eye contact. Since you do not have anything to read, you have to focus on the audience. Therefore, you can create a connection with the audience. You are free to move around. Again, with nothing in your hands, you are free to move closer or farther from the audience. You do not have to stand behind a podium or in one place to read the speech via a teleprompter. It is short and brief. Since you do not know what to say, you tend to be brief and to the point.

Disadvantages

You do not know what to say. Although you feel obligated to speak, you do not know what to say. You sit and think of the perfect speech. But when you get in front of the room, you forget what you wanted to say. Relax! It is okay. There are many others who wish they had the courage to speak in front of an audience. It is not organized. The speech is not organized with a proper introduction, body, and conclusion. You tend to sway. In order to not forget or to combat nervousness, people tend to sway from side to side. As if swaying, much as a metronome on a piano, will keep them on track to remember. You use vocal fillers such as um, ah, you know, are all non-words used to fill space when speaking. Why do people use vocal fillers instead of pausing? I have heard my students say it takes up space so you are not silent for too long. But how long does it take to say um? You can insert a pause of two or three seconds when speaking and still sound fluent. Little or no research. Since you did not have enough time to write this speech, it contains little or no research.

Recommendations

If you find yourself in a situation in which you have to deliver a speech using the impromptu method, relax. Remember, the audience does not know that you did not prepare or what you are going to say. Think of three or four areas you want to address and add a couple of stories. If you have to thank people, thank them in groups rather than as individuals. This way you would not forget to mention someone. An example would be "I would like to thank the nurses on the 4th floor ..." Stick to the subject and be brief. The longer you speak the more you risk the chance of going off on tangents and looking disorganized.

Extemporaneous

Extemporaneous is a method that uses an outline to deliver your speech. It is not the exact wording of the speech but a guide of what you want to say. Everything you say in the speech will not be written on the outline. Use keywords or phrases, not full sentences. This is a conversational style of speaking. The extemporaneous method combines the other methods. You have a partial manuscript because you have the outline of the speech. You are using your memory because not everything you are going to say will be on the outline. You are using the impromptu method because you can adjust by adding or taking away information based on the responses of the audience.

Advantages

The advantages are the same as the manuscript, memory, and impromptu. The extemporaneous method is a combination of the other methods. Therefore, it carries the same advantages and disadvantages as the manuscript, memory, and impromptu methods. It is a conversational style. Since you are not reading off a full text of the speech, but using keywords or phrases—your delivery will sound more natural, more conversational.

Adjust to audience feedback. This is the only method that allows you to adjust your presentation to the audience. You are asked to speak at a conference and prior to your presentation, the master of ceremonies said you have 20 minutes to speak. But once at the speaking site, the MC says you now have only 15 minutes. You can quickly cut something out of the speech and it will still flow smoothly. Likewise, if told you have more time you can add to your presentation. If an audience member asks a question, you can answer the question and continue with the presentation.

Disadvantages

Same as the manuscript, memory, and impromptu.

Recommendations

The extemporaneous method is the best method for delivering your speech. It is good for all speaking occasions because you can adapt it on the spot. Keep your outline brief with a limited amount of notes and note cards. Similar to the other methods, you must practice several times. Practice makes perfect. The notes are your guides as a reminder of what you want to speak about. Therefore, you should glance at your outline occasionally to get the information.

Now that you understand the various methods, let's turn our attention to the vocal delivery.

Vocal Delivery

Areas of Vocal Delivery

Vocal delivery includes the combination of volume, rate, pitch, articulation, and pronunciation. The nonverbal name is paralanguage. Your goal as a speaker is to use appropriate vocal variety to get your point across. Emphasize certain words to reinforce ideas and to speak with conviction. Your voice should be natural and spontaneous. So, let's look at each area.

The *volume* deals with the loudness or softness of your voice. Have you ever been at an event and cannot hear what the speaker is saying even though the speaker is speaking with a microphone? Well, this is because the speaker is speaking to the mic not the audience. Remember that you must always speak to those audience members in the back of the room. This ensures everyone will be able to hear what you are saying. If you only speak to the front of the room the people in the middle and back will not be able to hear you because your voice is not loud enough. Always adjust your volume to the size of and the noise level in the room. The more air you produce the louder you will speak, and the less air the softer.

Rate deals with the speed of your speaking. Varying your rate can indicate many things to the audience. If you speak too quickly, the audience will perceive you to be nervous and will not understand what you are saying. Similarly, if you speak too slowly, the audience will perceive that you are unsure of yourself and lack confidence and therefore will not want to listen to you speak. You will begin to bore them. Your rate needs to be so lively that the audience wants to hear what you have to say.

Pitch deals with the highness and lowness of your voice, tone, and voice quality. Some people have a naturally high pitch tone while others have a lower tone. If the pitch of your voice is too high, it will irritate the audience or the audience might perceive you as comical, such as actress Fran Drescher (*The Nanny*). Her nasal high pitch voice makes the character seem unwise and childish. Do not get me wrong; it is not my intention to insult anyone with a high-pitched voice. Due to media and stereotypical images presented, however, people will automatically associate a high pitch nasal voice with the character.

Articulation deals with producing speech sounds clearly and distinctly. Everyone has an accent. Accents are beautiful and have nothing to do with a person's intelligence. I have heard students mistakenly say to someone with an accent that the person needs to learn English. Regardless of your accent, as a speaker it is important to produce sound clearly and distinctly so the audience can understand your message.

Pronunciation deals with producing syllables of words according to an accepted standard. Some cultures say *to-ma-to* and others say *to-mat-o.*

When speaking, don't strain your voice. Do not whisper when your voice is strained or hoarse. Use a pleasant natural voice when addressing the audience. Your vocal delivery should not distract the audience but captivate and compel them. Talk to your audience and not at them by speaking in a conversational tone. Avoid using *well, ummmm, yeah,* or *ok* to start a sentence.

Common Mistakes

Monotone. This occurs because you lack vocal variety. You are not varying your rate, pitch, and volume. If you persist in speaking in a monotone manner the audience will not listen to you. Audience members might leave or fall asleep.

Too soft. This occurs when you speak to the people in the first row and do not project your voice to the back of the room. This manner of speaking indicates to audience members that you are nervous and not confident with them or the topic.

Too loud. This occurs when you yell at as if the audience were hard of hearing. When you yell, you will irritate your audience and it will stop listening.

Inappropriate pauses or no pauses. Inappropriate pauses occur when you do not know your presentation well, and no pauses occur when you are in a hurry to finish the presentation and sit down. The former alerts the audience that you are unsure about your topic while the latter alerts it of your nervousness.

Not fluent. This can occur because of nervousness or when you are not prepared. You will then tend to stutter or pause because you are unsure of your information.

Mispronunciation of words. It is importation to take the time to learn how to pronounce the major words in your presentation. While your audience might forgive one or two mispronounced words, it will not forgive many such errors.

Poor articulation. Omitting sounds, like *somethin'* instead of *something*; substituting sounds, such as *thang* for *thing.* This might occur because of culture influences. One way to solve this issue is to take a voice and diction class in your school.

Breathiness. This occurs due to nervousness. When you are nervous, your vocal cords tend to constrict. If you find that you are speaking from the throat and not your diaphragm, simply pause and take a deep breath to open up your vocal cords. Speaking in this manner will alert the audience of your nervousness.

Smacking of lips or sucking of teeth. This occurs again because of nervousness. Abundance of saliva is being produced in your mouth and you are swallowing it too hard. Take your time.

Mechanical. This occurs when you preplan the inflection of your voice to the point that it sounds unnatural and over-rehearsed. Be your natural self. No one wants to listen to a robot for too long.

Vocal Fillers. Yes, the *ummms*, *uhs*, *ok*, and *you knows* are some of the common vocal fillers that can kill your presentation and make you sound not credible. Why do you use vocal fillers? Why not just pause? Most people use vocal fillers because they feel they cannot be silent when speaking. But this is not the case. You can place a two- or three-second pause in the middle of a sentence and still have the speech flow smoothly. Plus, silence gives you time to think briefly about your next remark.

Non-vocal Delivery

Your presentation begins with the audience seeing you recognizing that you are the presenter. So your nonverbal communication should be considered at all times. Always approach the presentation area with confidence. When approaching the front of the room, do not stop to talk to individuals in the audience. Remember that others are waiting to hear from you. Do not start the speech while approaching the platform area. When you get to the speaking platform, set up in a professional manner to maintain your ethos. Before speaking, pause, review your notes, prepare yourself mentally, and start speaking to a pleasant person who is looking at you. If you don't find a pleasant face the first time, simply look back down again and find that pleasant face. If you start your presentation to someone who does not look interested, it will increase your anxiety. Always start your presentation in the front center of the room. Even if you are going to use PowerPoint for your attention getter, stand to the front center, pause so the audience may recognize you, and then move to the side to bring up the image. Do not rush into the opening sentence. To appear confident, walk to the front center of the room, take the time to look at the audience with a pleasant face, and start the presentation looking at them, not reading of your manuscript. Likewise once the presentation is over, pause briefly after you finish the presentation before leaving. Leave all notes and materials on the platform. You can get them later. Do not rush off the platform. Appreciate the audience applause. To understand how to polish your nonverbal behavior, let us look at some of the common speaker's mistakes.

Paralanguage

Paralanguage deals with your vocal variety, the changing of your rate, volume, and pitch to get your point across and to convey the essence of your speech. We addressed this in the section on the voice. So let's move on to the other nonverbal clues.

Eye Contact

You must look at the audience members in the eyes. This is very important for speakers to communicate to the audience through the eyes. It engages audience members and tells them they can trust you. The eyes are the mirrors to your soul. So engage your audience. Here are some common mistakes that people make.

Read too much. Have you ever seen a speaker reading verbatim from a manuscript? How does it make you feel? Do you feel unimportant to the speaker? Do you wish you were somewhere else? You tend not to trust the speaker because you think that he or she does not know the information.

Oscillating eyes from side to side. This occurs when the speaker is so stiff that he or she just moves the eyes from side to side. Oscillating eyes make it seem you are up to something, and again the audience cannot trust you. When you move your eyes, you should also move your head in the direction you are looking.

Looking at empty spaces. In a large room, you can get away with looking at empty spaces because the audience cannot see your eyes. In a smaller room, however, audience members will know you are not looking at them, leaving them to wonder what has your attention. Have you ever had someone describe something to you while looking in a particular direction? After a while, you start looking in the same direction as the speaker. You want the audience to focus on you, so look at them.

Looking at the ceiling or the floor. Some speakers will look up as they are speaking, as if the words were written on the ceiling. After a while, the audience will also begin to look up, and will not be concentrating on your speech. The same holds true for the speaker who looks at the floor.

Glancing too quickly. This occurs when the speaker looks up from reading for a few seconds to give the illusion he or she is looking at the audience. The audience is not fooled by this action. Again, they will think that you don't know your subject matter and will not trust the information.

Ignoring one side of the room. Speakers will sometimes turn their body sideways and only speak to one side of the room, leaving audience members feeling that the other side of the room is more important than them.

Using Eye Contact Effectively

As a speaker you should engage your audience. For a large audience of 100 or more, you can apply the inverted M or triangle methods.

The Inverted M. Look to the back of the room and then to the front. Now look to the right middle back, and then to the front. Continue these actions until you make an M.

Triangle method. Think about a triangle. Look to the bottom right corner of the room and then to the left corner of the room. Finally, look to the top of the room, thus creating a triangle with your eyes. These methods only work with a large audience. You will have to look at each member individually for a small audience. For smaller rooms, begin by looking at the middle and then move to the right, looking at different individuals for two or three sentences before proceeding to someone else. Take time to look at different individuals as you move back to the middle and then to the left of the room. Remember that if you want to establish a relationship with and have audience members trust you, you must look them in the eyes.

Facial Expressions

Facial expressions are the involuntary movements of the muscles in your face. Sometimes you can control them and sometimes your subconscious controls them. These uncontrolled expressions are called micro expressions. However, your facial expression should reinforce your ideas and emotions. But what are the mistakes speakers make with their expressions?

Not smiling. A smile says, *I like myself and I like you too.* A frown says just the opposite, *I hate myself and I hate you too.* Would you rather the audience like you or hate you? Your audience members will mimic your facial expressions. If you are speaking to a room of individuals who are frowning, it will increase your anxiety. You want your audience members to be supportive with their expressions. So smile!

Laughing in awkward places. Some people tend to laugh when they are nervous. Use this to your advantage and place some light humor throughout your speech. One thing about a joke is that if the audience does not laugh, then it did not know it was a joke and you can continue talking. Audience members will forgive you for laughing at your own humor, and this in turn will relax both you and them. Also, the audience will connect more with you because people like to laugh, and if you can get them laughing you will, in most cases, establish a positive relationship.

Making faces when you make a mistake. Some speakers will alert the audience that they have made a mistake by making a face or grimacing. Remember, the audience does not know your speech. Audience members only hear what you are delivering so if you make a mistake they will never know—unless you alert them. So, no funny faces.

Preplanned expressions. When you preplan your expressions, you appear fake and robotic. Your goal is to be as natural as possible when dealing with the audience.

Bobbing head. This occurs when you keep looking up and down very quickly, mimicking the bobble-head figure on a car dashboard whose head shakes every time the car moves.

Posture

The way you stand is very important. If your posture is correct, your voice projection will increase. Poor posture equals poor voice projection. Here are the common mistakes:

Rocking and swaying. Some speakers rock from side to side and back to front when speaking, appearing as if they are keeping rhythm with music. This shows the audience that the speaker is insecure and nervous. Adults do not sway. Children do when they are telling a lie or being scolded. You do not want the audience to associate you with a small child.

Pacing. When a speaker walks from side to side or back and forth, it tires the audience because they are working too hard for the information. After a while, they will stop looking at you. When you walk, you must walk with purpose and not aimlessly to overcome nervousness or to help you remember your speech.

2-step. This occurs when the speaker is hesitant to walk and steps from side to side. When walking you must take two or more steps. As I stated earlier, you should walk with a purpose. The best time to walk is during transitions. Therefore, start the introduction in the front center of the room, and then walk to the right as you begin to talk about the first point in the body of your speech. While on the right side of the room, pay more attention to the audience members on the left side of the room because they are the farthest from you. The individuals in the front have to focus on you because you are in their personal space. Then walk back to the center of the room when making the transition from the first main point to the second main point. The second point should be addressed in the middle of the room. Then walk during the transition from the second main point to the third main point. Now you are on the left side of the room so pay attention to the individuals on the right of the room. Remember that they are the farthest from you and need your attention too. You should walk back to the front center of the room for the conclusion. Remember, always start and end your presentation in the front center of the room.

Crossing legs. Do not cross your legs as if you have to go to the bathroom. Stand with both feet side by side with at least three inches between your feet.

Leaning from side to side. When you lean from one side to another, you will begin to sway. Keep both feet planted at least three inches apart. Do not lock your knees back because you need to be ready to walk if needed.

Gestures

The movements you make with your hands. Most novice speakers do not know what to do with their hands while speaking. They perform pressure gestures that alert the audience that they are nervous. These common gestures have interesting names:

1. Fig Leaf: When a speaker crosses his or her hands in front of the groin area. Thus, the name fig leaf. It is as if the speaker is trying to hide something.
2. Parade Rest: When a speaker crosses the hands behind the back as if in the military.
3. Sisters of Mercy: When speakers knit their fingers in front of them as if praying for divine inspiration.
4. Dead Fish Arms: This occurs when the speaker just lets the arms drop to the length of the body and does not move them.
5. Playing with Clothing or Jewelry: Sometimes a speaker will play with a ring or tug on clothes while talking. Some may even put a hand in a pocket and play with loose changes.
6. Slapping Body for Emphasis: This occurs when a speaker slaps his or her leg or chest when making a point.
7. Playing with Hair or Pushing it Aside: Such gestures again alert the audience that the speaker is nervous.

8. Programming Gestures: This occurs when a speaker practices a gesture so much that it appears robotic.
9. Wringing or rubbing your hands together.

The goal is to be natural. All your gestures should be made above the waist and in front of you for more emphasis. Always make sure your elbows are bent and your palms are open when making gestures. Yes, do make gestures. It is only natural that you do so when making your presentation. Do not point at the audience. It is considered rude and offensive by some cultures. If you do not know what to do with your hands, do the steeple gesture. This is when you create a church-like steeple with your hands, with fingertips touching. When you look at your hands you see a triangle. This tells the audience that you are confident and that they can trust you.

FIGURE 4.1.

Index Cards

To help you deliver the speech, you can place the information on index cards, a teleprompter, or a tablet. If you are required to use index cards, here are some common mistakes:

1. Bending the cards. You might be tempted to bend or roll them as you play with the cards.
2. Waving of the cards. If you hold the index cards in your dominant hand, you will have a tendency to wave and point them at the audience. You should hold them in your less dominant hand. Therefore, if you are a right-handed person, hold them in your left hand. Likewise, if you are a left-handed person, hold them in your right hand. This way you will not wave or point them at the audience.
3. Slapping of the cards. Again, when people are nervous they tend to slap the cards because it gives them something to do with their hands. The cards should be held in your hand close to the body, as if it is an extension of you. When you need to look at a card, simply push it forward and look at the card, and then return it to the resting place.
4. Writing on both sides of a card. This will introduce more communication noise into the speaking setting because the audience will try to read what you have on the back of the card.
5. Having cards in an improper order. Always check your cards before you begin your presentation to ensure they are in the right order.
6. Using cards that are not white. Sometimes you might be tempted to use various colored cards. Do not use them. Use plain white cards. Using colored cards will introduce noise into the communication setting.
7. Using cards that are too large. Sometimes the speaker might be tempted to use large cards because they will hold more information. The best-sized cards to use are 3" × 5" because they can fit into your hands without having too much protruding out. If you use a large card, it will make it easier for the audience to see your hands shaking.

8. Handwritten/sloppy cards. In the world of higher learning, handwritten work is not appropriate. Never turn in sloppy, crossed-out work to your professor.

Remember, regardless of the method you use for your outline, it should not distract from the presentation. Index cards should be small, white, and held in a manner that does not distract the audience.

Attire

How you look and carry yourself is important to your presentation. Remember you are representing your own brand. Your audience will make a judgment on your ethos based on your verbal and also your nonverbal communication, which includes your appearance. When in front of an audience your attire should be on the same level or one level above your audience. If they are in business casual, you can be in business causal or business attire. You should never be a level below your audience, as this will diminish your ethos. Your dress should complement not distract from your presentation. It should be tasteful, professional, neat, clean, pressed, and it should fit properly. There are some common mistakes men and women make when delivering their presentations:

Men's Mistakes

1. Not well groomed. Speakers must always be well groomed. What is well groomed? From your head to your feet, you should be neat and professional appearing. Your hair, including any facial hair, should be combed and neatly shaven. Preferably, your face should be clean-shaven because in the U.S. business world this relates to trust. No facial hair means you are open and trustworthy. Your clothing should be clean, well fitted, and wrinkle free.
2. Wrong shoes. Sneaker, work boots, and loafers are more business casual. The type of shoes that are more business professional are Windsor Wingtip Oxford lace-up shoes. Your shoes should be preferably black or brown, with leather soles and properly shined.
3. Wrinkled clothing. Nothing will decrease your ethos quicker than wearing wrinkled clothing. Always make sure the material of your suit and shirts are wrinkle free.
4. Busy tie/no tie. Proper business attire includes a tie. Your tie should not create communication noise by having too much pattern or images on the tie. It should be simple and plain. Red is the color of power. So, you can introduce power into your outfit with a red tie. Likewise, blue is the color of credibility.
5. Clothing too tight/loose. You do not want to look as if you borrowed your suit from your father or little brother. Make sure the suit is tailored for your body frame. A European cut is more tailored for a smaller, longer image. It does not work with everyone.

Putting Together a Business Wardrobe

Every man's closet should have a basic navy blue and black suit. You want a navy blue suit because blue is considered the color of credibility. Alan Vinson (2014) in the article entitled "Why the Color of your Suit Matters" offers great advice on when to wear certain colors. Be careful when you pick a black suit that you don't resemble a mortician.

You should have a basic white and light blue wrinkle-free shirt and a red tie. Once you have the basic color then you can add a gray or pinstripe suit. Stay away from brown because this is a color that does not excite the eyes. Red is the color that excites, and the way to get it into your outfit is through your tie. As cited earlier, you need a basic black and brown lace-up shoes with matching socks and belt.

Women's Mistakes

1. Clothing too tight or short. The goal of your presentation is to get the audience to listen to your presentation and not be distracted by your outfit. Your clothes should be fitted to your body, frame high on the top and low on the bottom. No prom dresses. High on the top and low on the bottom. If you have to ask whether it is appropriate, then it is probably not.
2. Wrong shoes. Sandals are business casual shoes. You want to wear pumps with 2 to 3-inch heels. You can get away with peep toe pumps. Be careful that your shoes do not look like you are going to the club. You should have your basic black-patent leather pumps.
3. Wrong stocking. Fishnet or colored stockings that match your clothes are not appropriate business professional attire. You want to wear stockings that match your skin tone or are sheer black.
4. Large jewelry. Do not wear jewelry that will distract the audience. If your earrings are too big or move every time you move, it will be a distraction. You want smaller pieces or pearls. Be careful not to wear too many bangles because they will make noise every time you move your arms. Less is best!
5. Hair covering eyes/face. Do not have your hair covering your face or eyes. Remember, the eyes are the mirrors to the soul. You want the audience to be able to look at your face and eyes. Having your hair covering your face and/or eyes will give the audience the impression that you are nervous, untrustworthy, or hiding something. Keep your hair away from your face and comb neatly.
6. Loud makeup. Your makeup should not arrive before you. You need to distinguish the difference between day and night makeups. Keep it simple. Again, you do not want anything that will distract the audience from your message.

Time

Time is money. Therefore, as a speaker, you must be able to adhere to the time limitations. If you are the guest speaker at an event and you do not stick to the scheduled time, your action can cause the event sponsor to pay more money to keep the venue longer. As such, do not make these common mistakes:

1. Most speakers do NOT pre-time their presentations. You must always time your presentation when you are practicing to know the length. Read the speech out loud as you will be delivering it, and time it several times so you will have an accurate time. Do not leave it to chance because you might find yourself speaking under or over the time limit. Both can cause you negative consequences. You might not be asked to speak at the venue again. Your professor might give you a lower grade because you did not meet the requirements of an assignment. If you were given a five- to six-page assignment and you turned in three pages, what grade would you receive? Be honest. The same holds true for your speech.

If you have to present a five- to six-minute speech and you deliver a three-minute speech, what grade should you get? Yes, an F. Why? Because 1) it is not what the professor requested, 2) it does not meet the requirements of the assignment, and 3) it is not fully developed.

2. Most speakers do NOT look at the timer while presenting. You must always look at the clock or timer so you do not go over or under the time requirements.
3. Most speakers do NOT pace themselves when presenting. It is important that you pace yourself while you are speaking. You should know where you should be after the first minute. If you are behind, then you know you have to speed up so you do not come in over the time limit. If you are too far in front, you will have to slow down to avoid coming in under the time. So pace yourself and look at the timer.
4. Most speakers do NOT start the conclusion with 30 seconds left. Most speakers underestimate how long or short a period this represents. Thirty seconds is just enough time to wrap up your speech. So when you see 30 seconds left, you should get to your conclusion. Remember that the audience does not know your written speech. It only knows what you tell it.
5. Most speakers do NOT stop when the time is finished. When your time is up, you should end your presentation. Do not say, "I am running out of time so I have to wrap up or I cannot finish." People do not like to think they are not getting all the information. Again, by doing this you will introduce communication noise in the communication setting. The audience will think about what it missed and not about the wonderful presentation you gave.

Therefore, remember that the delivery of the speech is 65%–90% of what you are communicating. It is not what you say but how you say it. Take the time to practice! Practice! Practice! But do not overdo it so that you become too stiff or robotic. Your goal is to be natural but professional and polished. You want to have a conversation with each member of the audience. Your delivery should be dynamic and passionate. The audience must believe that you are passionate about your topic and your presentation. We were all born with the ability to communicate but practice makes almost perfect!

Confident

Why are you nervous or afraid of Public speaking? Most people are afraid of speaking in public because they fear humiliation, they lack preparation, they are worried about their image, they lack experience, or they fear failure. These are all in your mind because of the pressure you put on yourself. Remember our definition of fear as False Evidence Appearing Real. You turn it on and you can turn it off. When you are at a wedding and they open the mic for people to speak, most people immediately become nervous. Once the open mic is closed, the nervousness leaves. The challenge is that you mind evaluates the situation and adrenaline begins to flow. In actuality, your mind has prepared you to fight, so you are very powerful. It is a natural experience, but we evaluate it and make it negative. So we take flight or don't participate. The mind is very powerful. It can make you sick when you are well, and it can make you well when you are sick. We have heard the stories of the doctor informing patients that they have a terminal illness and the person set their mind that the disease will not beat them. Then later, with treatment, the disease is in remission. We have also heard about the person who gets the same diagnosis and, because they take a defeatist attitude, the disease accelerates and they die early. No one knows for sure what happened in these cases, but Beecher's initial research in "The Powerful Placebo" has shown through the pseudo effect that the mind is a powerful thing (1955). So you have to condition your mind. How can you do this? You are most nervous when you get the assignment, right before you speak, at the beginning of the presentation, and sometimes when you are writing your presentation. But you should understand when you start the presentation that you are more nervous than you look. Every speaker experiences some form of nervousness. In his Ted talk "No Freaking Speaking: Managing Public Speaking Anxiety," Matt Abrahams (2012) identified three sources of anxiety: situation based, audience based, and goal based. So what can you do to build you confidence? Don't procrastinate. As soon as you get the assignment, get started. Follow the guidelines in chapters one and two for getting started and writing the speech. Recreate the speaking environment at home and practice! practice! practice! Here are some helpful dos and don'ts to assist you with anxiety while speaking.

Dos
Before Presenting:

1. Visualize your success. Arrive early and see the audience responding positively to you.
2. Give yourself a mental pep talk. Example: "Everyone wants to hear me. They will love my presentation! I'm prepared, and I'm confident. I know what I am doing. This is my best presentation ever."
3. Get your mind creating: Do some activities. Example: You can breathe in while counting 1 and breath out counting 1, 2. Then breath in while counting 1, 2 and breathe out while counting 1, 2, 3, 4. Keep going, doubling the numbers as you go. The mind is now focused on creating the numbers and not evaluating the situation. Plus, the breathing will help to open your lungs so you can project out.

Right before you speak:

1. Pause briefly before to check that everything is ready.
2. Mentally review the first few sentences in the introduction.
3. Take a deep breath.
4. Smile, and have a conversation with your audience. Don't talk at them! Talk to them! Use conversational language (personal pronouns like you, we, us) and rhetorical questions to connect with the audience.
5. Look for a positive listener to start talking to.

After you speak:

1. Pause, and appreciate the audience applause.
2. Focus on what you did well, not any mistakes.
3. Tell yourself something positive. Example: I did it! It was great! You are the best!
4. Celebrate your success. Example: Drink your favorite drink, or eat your favorite food. Give someone a high five. Laugh, smile, and enjoy your accomplishment.

Don't
Before presenting

1. Do not talk about being nervous. There have been many times I was in the elevator and heard students talking about how nervous they are about an exam or a presentation. Do fall into this trap because you do not want to fall prey to the self fulfilling prophesy. Your mind thinks, "Oh well, he/she wants to fail.

Let me help him/her." Remember the saying, "if you think you can or you think you cannot, you are both right.

While presenting

1. Don't rush into starting.
2. Don't focus on your fears; it will tighten them.
3. Don't quit: If things are going wrong, do not walk off the platform. Simply pause take a deep breath and continue.

After presenting

1. Don't focus on your mistakes.
2. Don't put down your presentation. The audience might think you did well.

Credit

- Fig. 4.1: Copyright © 2016 Depositphotos/stevanovicigor.

CHAPTER 5

Outlining

A lot of people believe they should memorize their speech. Unfortunately, this is not the best method to deliver your presentation. Do not memorize your speech because you will sound robotic, and if you make a mistake the whole speech is thrown off. The best method of delivering your speech is extemporaneous, in which you use an outline to guide you throughout the presentation. The advantages of delivering your speech from an outline are that you will be able to adapt the speech to match the audience's response while also allowing you to engage the audience. It is up to the speaker to determine whether he or she will use a formal or informal outline. A formal outline contains Roman numerals, capital letters, and even numbers arranged in a tiered, hierarchical pattern. The informal outline contains bulleted or numbered items or simply a series of notes to help you organize your ideas and research.

For either informal or formal outlines, you can choose between either a topic outline, in which the details are written in phrases, or a sentence outline, in which the details are written in complete sentences. In the formal outline, use only phrases or sentences but not both.

When writing a speech, use the formal sentence outline. When practicing the speech, use the formal phase outline. And when delivering your speech, use a formal key word outline.

To develop your outline, you should understand the outline sequence.

Outline Sequence

The following is the standard accepted sequences of symbols for outlining:

I. Main point
  A. Sub point of I
    1. Sub point of A
      a. Sub point of 1
        (1) Sub point of a
          (a) Sub point of (1)

Roman numerals are used for your main points. Each of the sub points is followed with capital letters. These main point sub points are followed by numbers, and the numbers are followed by lowercase letters.

An example of a formal sentence outline might be: I. It is important to understand the ingredients needed to bake a carrot cake. (indent) A. You will need a certain amount of wet material. (indent) B. You will need to gather your dry materials.

With an understanding of the symbols, let us turn our attention to the guidelines you should follow to ensure your outline is correct.

1. Use the correct symbols, which are Roman numerals (I), capital letters (A), numbers (2), and lowercase letters (a). It is important that you use them in the correct order listed. The following are the standard accepted sequences of symbols for outlining:

   I. Main point
     A. Sub point of I
       1. Sub point of A
         a. Sub point of 1
           (1) Sub point of a
             (a) Sub point of (1)

2. Each sub point must have at least two subdivisions, if any. For instance:
   - Every I must have a II
   - Every A must have a B
   - Every 1 must have a 2
   - Every a must have a b

An Example of Subdivision

This

I.
    A.
        1.
        2.
    B.
    C.
        1.
            a.
            b.
        2.
II.

Not This

1.
    A.
        1.
    B.
    C.
        1.
            a.

The sequence on the left is correct. The sequence on the right is incorrect. Can you spot the mistakes? If you said that the #2 sub point of A, the lowercase b sub point of C1, and the #2 of sub point C are missing, you are correct. Think of it this way. If you have an apple and you cut in it half, how many parts do you have?

3. The same holds true for subdivisions. If you have to create a sub point, you must have at least two parts or you did not have to create a sub point. An example:

I. Types of dogs
    A. Poodle
    B. German Shepherd

But if I wanted to have a sub point for each dog category, there must be at least two sub points.

I. Types of dogs
    A. Poodle
        1. Fur
        2. Color

    B. German Shepherd

4. You must indent properly.

1. Every speech has three parts
    A. The first part is the introduction

    B. The second part
    is the body **(NOT THIS)**

    C. The third part is the
    conclusion **(NOT THIS)**

5. You should capitalize the first word of each point.
6. Begin the introduction, the body, and the conclusion with Roman numeral I. Treat each of the three major parts as a complete unit.

THIS	**NOT THIS**
Introduction	Introduction
I.	**I.**
II.	II.
III.	III.
IV	IV.
V	V.
Body	Body
I.	**VI.**
II.	VII.
III.	VIII.
Conclusion	Conclusion
I.	**IX.**
II	IIX.

7. Use one discrete idea or sentence for each symbol. This is a common mistake most students make because they want to write the entire speech in the form of a manuscript and place symbols next to the sentences wherever needed. But this is not the purpose of an outline. Remember that the outline is a brief guide of what you want to say. Everything you say should not be written on the outline. If it is, then you are using both the manuscript and extemporaneous methods. For example:

THIS
I. A small business can make more money if the staff is better trained.
II. A small business can make more money if the staff is highly motivated.

NOT THIS
I. A small business can make more money if it trains its staff better and if the staff is highly motivated.

8. You should use simple sentences or phrases. Again, your outline is just a guide of what you want to say.

THIS
I. Children should be raised by the state.
A. Equality for children
B. Parents released for work.

OR
I. Children should be raised by the state.
A. All children treated equally.
B. Parents released to work.

9. You should not wave or bend the cards. It is easy to play with the note cards when you are nervous. Use the technique in the chapter on delivery to assist you in using the cards properly.
10. You should practice using the index cards. Most people make the mistake of practicing the speech from a manuscript and not the note cards. If you do this then you run the risk of your delivery not being fluent. These are two very distinct methods that required different strategies.
11. You must look at the audience more than the index cards. Ninety percent of your delivery must be directed at the audience. Remember, your goal is to connect and to have a conversation with the audience. You cannot do this if you are reading. This is the reason for using an outline.
12. You should highlight materials you have difficulty recalling. Have you ever practiced a speech and every time you look up and then look down you cannot find your place? It is as if your mind is playing a trick on you because it occurs in the same place. Well, take a highlighter and mark the first word in the sentence that you have difficulty recalling. Of course, it does not work if you have to highlight every sentence in the speech. But this is a neat trick to aid your delivery.
13. You can add delivery cues/reminders on your cards to assist you in your delivery or to relax or remind you of what to do. Some common delivery clues are "slow down," "pause," and "relax."
14. You should include all citations on the cards. By including the citation you avoid plagiarism while it also serves as a reminder to state the reference while delivering your presentation. It is important that you state your references within the delivery of the speech to increase your ethos in the minds of audience members.
15. You should number the note cards, just in case you drop them and need to quickly place them back into the right order.
16. You should type your words in a font size large enough for you to see them. Do not make the mistake of typing the information so small that it crams everything on the card and you cannot read it.

Helpful Delivery Hints

Sample Index Cards Setup for the Outline

Name Card #1

The following is the information you should collect for your references when you use electronic sources if using APA style:

- Author's name
- Year of publication
- Title of the document
- Date the site was accessed
- Sponsoring institution or organization
- Title of the website
- The URL, including the protocol, domain name, domain type, directory path, and file name
- If the DOI (digital object identifier) is present, you don't need the URL.

The Sample speech outline for index cards

Introduction

- I. Road map story
- II. To inform about outlining
- III. Reference about outlining importance
- IV. Outlining advantages
    - A. Organization
    - B. Rehearsal
    - C. Revise

- V. Three Principles
    - A. Headings
    - B. Formatting
    - C. Rules

Body

- I. Four headings (simple format)
    - A. Name first card
    - B. Introduction—first card in the center
    - C. Body—second card in the center
    - D. Conclusion—fifth card in the center

Now with an understanding of how to compose your heading, you will need to understand standard outlining format.

- II. The format (more structure)
    - A. Roman numerals for main points
        - 1. Capital letters—Sub points
        - 2. Arabic numerals—Sub sub points
        - 3. Lower case letters—further subdivision
    - B. Division of points
        - 1. II to match I
        - 2. B to match A
        - 3. 2 to match 1
        - 4. b to match a
    - C. Main point transitions
        - 1. Bottom line of the card
        - 2. Helps flow

Now that I have informed you about standard outline format, I will inform you about the rules for outlining.

- III. Outlining Rules (very detailed)
    - A. Introduction body and conclusion
        - 1. Roman numerals section

2. Introduction function
   a) Attention Getter
   b) Thesis
   c) Reason to listen
   d) Credibility
   e) Preview
3. Body functions
4. Conclusion function
   a) Summarize
   b) Reinforce
   c) Close

B. One sentence per letter/number
C. Distinct ideas
D. List:
   1. Ingredients, etc.
   2. Part of a larger whole
   3. Awkward or unnatural sentences
E. Citing sources in the text
   1. Authors name
   2. Date
   3. Example (American Psychological Association, 1990)
F. Directly quoting, page number
   4. Authors name
   5. Date
   6. Page #
   7. Example (American Psychological Association, 1990, p. 69)
G. Use only 3 index cards for the body

Conclusion

I. Three principles
   A. Headings
   B. Formatting
   C. Rules
II. Know importance
III. Great road map

Reference

American Psychological Association (1990). Publication Manual of American Psychological Association (4th ed.). Washington, D.C.

CHAPTER 6

Presentational Aids

"A picture is worth a thousand words." How true! To make your presentation more effective, you need to include presentational aids. They will help your audience understand what you are saying. Presentational aids have a life and dynamics that, when used well, will enhance your presentation. However, if they are not used well, they will kill your presentation. So let's now turn our attention to helping you understand, create, and use presentational aids effectively.

Functions of Aids

Not every speech calls for you to have presentational aids. It is important to know when you need to use presentational aids and the role of presentational aids. Listed below are some core functions of your aids:

- It gains and maintains the audience's attention. A well-structured aid will grab your audience's attention and keep them interested in your presentation.
- It enhances the audience's understanding of your topic. If you try to describe how to juggle three balls, it will confuse the audience if you do not show how to do it.
- It enhances the audience's memory. The audience might not remember everything you said, but they will remember seeing an image of a sick child or feeling the soft fur of a rabbit.
- It helps the audience organize ideas and procedures. It is much better to show the audience how to make a pineapple upside-down cake than just to describe it. The audience will be able to understand the step-by-step process.
- It reinforces your message. Again, if you were describing the devastating effects of Hurricane Sandy, it would be better to show images to your audience.

Now that you know why you use presentational aids, we can look at the types of presentational aids available to you.

Types of Aids

There are many forms of aids you can choose:

- Objects
- People
- Models
- Drawings
- Photographs
- Maps
- Graphs
- Movies
- Music

These forms of visual aids can be placed on slideware, such as Prezi, Microsoft PowerPoint, Apple iWork Keynote, Google Slides etc., posterboards, or some form of paper. They can be displayed using computers, portfolios, SmartBoard, Whiteboard, or Chalkboard and Flip Charts. Or you can stream them or share them by using such program as ZOOM, SlideShark.

Objects—These are the actual objects. If you are going demonstrate to your audience how to make a red velvet cake, you will need to bring in the ingredients and tools necessary to make the cake. Also, make sure that your objects are large enough and clear enough for the audience to see. You should use see-through containers, so the audience can see the mixtures. Remember, the goal is for the audience to learn—nothing frustrates an audience more than not being able to see or hear your presentation.

Models—Sometimes you cannot use the actual object, so you will use a model or replica of the actual object. For instance, if you are demonstrating how to brush your teeth properly, I would not expect you to get up in front of the room to demonstrate on yourself. The audience would be disgusted to see you brushing and spitting. Instead, you could bring the large dentures you find in a dentist's office, and use them for your demonstration. Your model should be appropriate in size and shape. One of my former students used a Barbie doll to demonstrate the proper technique to diaper a baby. Using a Barbie doll instead of a baby doll immediately reduced his ethos and made his presentation feel commercial.

People—You can ask for volunteers to assist you with your presentation. For instance, if you want to demonstrate how to apply makeup, it would be difficult to do it on yourself without a mirror; however, the mirror might block your demonstration. Instead, you could use a volunteer. It is important when you use a volunteer that you prep them before the presentation. I have seen volunteers ruin students' presentations because they did not know what to do. Don't have volunteers sitting aimlessly in front of the audience when you are not using them. Place them in the audience, and call them to the front when you are ready to use them. Once you are finished, have them return to their seat. This will ensure that the audience is focused on you and that your volunteer does not look or feel awkward.

Drawings, photographs, maps, and charts—These must be large, simple, and clear. When using maps, it is best to use the silhouette of the maps because they are simple and easy to follow to show location and size. Make sure to properly cite all materials taken from another source.

Dos

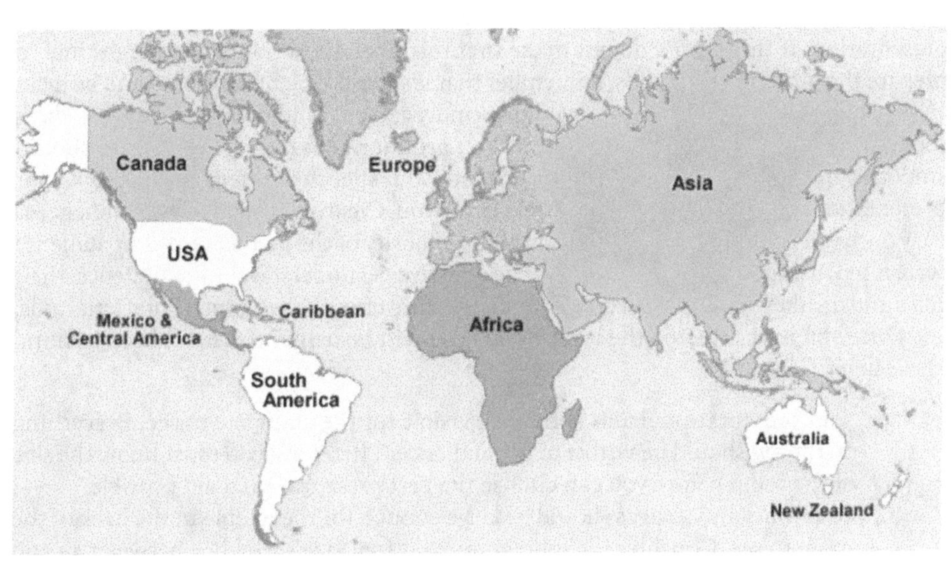

FIGURE 6.1a.

Don'ts

FIGURE 6.1b.

Movies and Music—Use short excerpts of no more than three to four minutes. Explain why you are using them and how they relate to your topic. Do not play them too long, or you will lose the attention and focus of the audience.

Guidelines for Developing Aids

Most speakers mistakenly believe they can create a dynamic aid the night before the presentation. If this is you, do not make that mistake. Allow yourself enough time to prepare the presentational aids. Remember that it should look professional and be neat. In general, it should not appear that a prekindergarten child created it. With today's technology, however, some pre-graders can produce amazing artwork. You should smoothly integrate the presentational aids into your speech. Remember to design your presentational aid for your audience and not for you. Creating the aid for the audience is easy once you do your audience analysis. If the majority of the members of your audience were blind, using PowerPoint would not be effective. So understand your audience, their likes and dislikes, culture, and demographics before choosing your presentational aids.

Once you have selected the type of aids you will be using, you must keep in mind these helpful tips.

1. Your presentational aids should be visible for the audience to see. Everything on the aid should be visible to the audience. Therefore, you must know the size of the room before you can choose the best presentational aid possible.
2. Your fonts and images should be large enough for the people in the back of the room to see. Consider the following: Your font size should be between 44 and 28 points. Below 28 points will be too small for the audience to see in a large room. Seventy-two points, unless it is a single-word title on a separate slide, will be too big.
3. Always check your slideware on the projector or SMART board, not the computer. On the computer, it will appear to be the right size; the projector or SMART board will provide an exact measurement, and you will not run the risk of the audience not seeing your slideware correctly.
4. Also, your aids should be simple. Do not over crowd your work area or your slides with too many images or writing. You should use short phrases and key words—not sentences. Remember you are the presenter. The audience should look to you for the information, not to the aid. If you do, the audience will not be able to focus on what you are saying. Audience members will have wandering eyes and will look at the things that attract them. Thus, you will lose the effectiveness of the aids and will instead be introducing more communication noise into the setting.

Too much information on a slide
When writing a speech, there are three parts of the speech you must have.
You must have the first part which is the introduction of the speech
You must have the second part which is the second part is the body of the speech
You must have the third part which is the conclusion of the speech

Too little information on a slide
Three parts of speech

Introduction
Body
Conclusion

Just enough information on a slide
The three part of the speech
The first part is the introduction
The second part the body
The third part is the conclusion

You are the presenter, and the audience must look to you for the information. Use short phrases.

5. If you are using slideware, keep in mind the three by three rule. No more than three images, phrases, words, fonts, and colors on any one slide. Simple aids are better than crowded aids. Follow the KISS rule—Keep It Short and Sweet.
6. If you are doing a demonstration speech, instead of having materials all over the table, arrange them in such a way that you can control the flow of information.

Color Choices

Using the correct color or theme is important. When choosing your colors always think contrast. Warm colors such as oranges and reds tend to come forward and excite people. Use these colors when you have exciting news. On the contrary, cool colors such as greens and blues tend to recede and have a calming effect. Therefore, use them for bad news. Think about a hospital. What colors are the recovery and patient rooms painted? They are usually white or cool colors. Imagine waking up from surgery in a red room. But where are all the warm colors? They are in the children's ward to keep their spirits up. Avoid red-green combinations in your presentation because they do not contrast well. Plus, some people in your audience might have color blindness.

For Computer-Generated Aids

Whenever you are creating slideware, using software such as PowerPoint (PPT), think contrast. It is best to use light text on dark backgrounds or dark text on light backgrounds. David JP Phillips in his TED Talk, "How to Avoid Death by PowerPoint," offers advice on creating PowerPoint based on the psychology of the brain. He presents five principles to help you enhance your PowerPoint slides:

1. One message per slide: People can only concentrate/focus on one thing effectively at a time.
2. Working memory: The redundancy effect states that if you have long sentences in your PowerPoint, and you speak at the same time you show the slides to the audience, it will NOT remember anything. Use short text and a simple image.

3. Size: People focus on four things: moving object, signaling colors (reds, greens, yellows), contrast-rich objects, and big objects. In most PowerPoint usage, the headline is the most prominent object on the slides. The most important part of your PPT should be the biggest contrast.
4. Contrast: Use contrast to present your information. Bring up the information as you are talking about it. Also, the background should be dark, not light, because you should be the biggest contrast. You are the presentation.
5. Objects: No more than six objects on any slides because you can easily see six. If you have more than six, the audience will have to count and use 500% more cognitive resources to understand the slide. Therefore, it will NOT pay attention. Use more slides for your presentation.

Guidelines for Using Aids

Now that you have created your presentational aids, consider these guidelines to presenting them:

Practice your presentation using the aids. Practicing with the aids will allow you to adjust and use your aids effectively.

Before starting your presentation check to make sure your aid is working properly, that you have all the needed materials, that the volume is on, that the pointer is working, that your PPT is in play mode, etc.

Start the speech front and center. Unless you are starting with the aid, always start your presentation in the front center of the room so that the audience focuses on you.

Use blank slides where needed. Start your PPT with a blank slide. This will keep your audience focused on you, not the slide. To keep its focus throughout, place blank slides where needed.

Show your aid when ready to explain it, and remove when finished explaining. This is where the blank slides are important. If you are finished with a slide and you are addressing another topic before the next slide, then place a blank between the two slides. This way the audience will be forced to look and focus on you.

Point to the aids as you explain the information. Do not just show the slides. You should explain the information on your slides. If you are using objects, hold the items high as you explain them.

Always face the audience as you talk to it, not the aid. Too often the speaker will face the SMART board or the volunteer instead of the audience, thus breaking his or her relationship with the audience. If you are demonstrating something, make sure your back is not turned to the audience.

Indicate on your outline va1, va2, etc., so that you do not forget to show or explain them.

When doing a demonstration speech do NOT use any dangerous or illegal aids. This will reduce your ethos in the mind of the audience. Also, keep the finished product until the end for greater effect.

Do not give audience members handouts before the presentation because you cannot control what they do with it. It is always best to give handouts at the end of your presentation. It is best, however, to have prepared aids.

Remember Murphy's Law—anything that can go wrong will go wrong. So be prepared. Always ask for a technician to be present when presenting. If something happens, do not attempt to fix the equipment. If you do and you cannot fix it, the audience will blame you for the faulty equipment and you will diminish your ethos. If the technician cannot fix it, the audience will blame him or her for ruining your presentation.

Using presentation aids will enhance your presentation if you develop and use them correctly. The audience will remember your presentation long after your delivery.

Credits

- Fig. 6.1a: Source: https://geology.com/world/world-map-clickable.gif.
- Fig. 6.1b: Copyright © 2015 Depositphotos/dikobrazik.

REFERENCES

Chen, D., & Haviland-Jones, J. (2000). Human Olfactory Communication of Emotion. *Perceptual and Motor Skills*. https://doi.org/10.2466/pms.2000.91.3.771

Evan Andrews. (2016). What is the origin of the handshake? Retrieved July 23, 2018, from https://www.history.com/news/what-is-the-origin-of-the-handshake

Hall, E. T. (1959). The silent language. In *The Silent Language*. https://doi.org/10.1007/s13398-014-0173-7.2

Jeff Haden. (2018). Yes, Thomas Edison Actually Made Job Candidates Try a Bowl of Soup Before He Would Hire Them | Inc.com. Retrieved July 23, 2018, from https://www.inc.com/jeff-haden/yes-thomas-edison-actually-made-job-candidates-try.html

Samovar, L. A., & Porter, R. E. (1988). *Intercultural Communication : A Reader* (5th ed.). Belmont, CA: Wadsworth Pub. Co.

Sloan, N. L., Ahmed, S., Anderson, G. C., & Moore, E. (2011). Comment on: "Kangaroo mother care" to prevent neonatal deaths due to pre-term birth complications. *International Journal of Epidemiology*. https://doi.org/10.1093/ije/dyq174

Stewart, G. L., Dustin, S. L., Barrick, M. R., & Darnold, T. C. (2008). Exploring the Handshake in Employment Interviews. *Journal of Applied Psychology*. https://doi.org/10.1037/0021-9010.93.5.1139

Suman Rao, P. N., Udani, R., Nanavati, R., Suman, R. P. N., Udani, R., & Nanavati, R. (2008). Kangaroo mother care for low birth weight infants: A randomized controlled trial. *Indian Pediatrics*.

Chen, D., & Haviland-Jones, J. (2000). Human Olfactory Communication of Emotion. *Perceptual and Motor Skills*. https://doi.org/10.2466/pms.2000.91.3.771

Evan Andrews. (2016). What is the origin of the handshake? Retrieved July 23, 2018, from https://www.history.com/news/what-is-the-origin-of-the-handshake

Hall, E. T. (1959). The silent language. In *The Silent Language*. https://doi.org/10.1007/s13398-014-0173-7.2

Jeff Haden. (2018). Yes, Thomas Edison Actually Made Job Candidates Try a Bowl of Soup Before He Would Hire Them | Inc.com. Retrieved July 23, 2018, from https://www.inc.com/jeff-haden/yes-thomas-edison-actually-made-job-candidates-try.html

Samovar, L. A., & Porter, R. E. (1988). *Intercultural Communication : A Reader* (5th ed.). Belmont, CA: Wadsworth Pub. Co.

Sloan, N. L., Ahmed, S., Anderson, G. C., & Moore, E. (2011). Comment on: "Kangaroo mother care" to prevent neonatal deaths due to pre-term birth complications. *International Journal of Epidemiology*. https://doi.org/10.1093/ije/dyq174

Stewart, G. L., Dustin, S. L., Barrick, M. R., & Darnold, T. C. (2008). Exploring the Handshake in Employment Interviews. *Journal of Applied Psychology*. https://doi.org/10.1037/0021-9010.93.5.1139

Suman Rao, P. N., Udani, R., Nanavati, R., Suman, R. P. N., Udani, R., & Nanavati, R. (2008). Kangaroo mother care for low birth weight infants: A randomized controlled trial. *Indian Pediatrics*.

Hall, E. T. (1959). The silent language. In E. G. (Ed.), *The Silent Language* (pp. 73–76). Fawcett Publications. https://doi.org/10.1007/s13398-014-0173-7.2

Hall, E. T. (1966). *The hidden dimension*. Garden City, NY: Doubleday.

Hall, E. T. (1979). *Beyond Culture*. Garden City, NY: Anchor.

Hecht, M. L., Anderson, P. A., & Ribeau, S. A. (1989). *The cultural dimensions of nonverbal communication*. In M. K. Asante & W. B. Gudykunst (Eds.), *Handbook of international and intercultural communication* (pp. 163–185). Newbury Park, CA: Sage.

Helmstetter, S. (1987). *What to say when you talk to yourself.* New York, NY: Pocket Books.

Hovland, C. I. (1957). *The order of presentation in persuasion*. New Haven, CT: Published for the Institute of Human Relations by Yale University Press.

Lincoski Jr., J. T. (2000). Sharing is Caring. Justia Trademarks. Retrieved August 2, 2018 from https://trademarks.justia.com/761/80/sharing-is-caring-76180417.html

McCroskey, J. C. (1968). *An Introduction to rhetorical communication*. Englewood Cliffs, NJ: Prentice-Hall.

Merriam–Webster. Process. Retrieved August 8, 2018 from URL: https://www.merriam-webster.com/dictionary/process

Morgan, M. (2009, July 6). Mass Communication: Types of Mass Communication [Video file]. Retrieved August 8, 2018 from https://ww.youtube.com/watch?v=JBHQZbCvcoo

Pappas, S. (2014). 5 Ways Your Emotions Influence Your World (and Vice Versa). Retrieved July 23, 2018 from https://www.livescience.com/43196-emotions-influence-perception.html

Philips, D. J. (2014, April 14) How to avoid death By PowerPoint [Video file]. Retrieved August 8, 2018 from https://www.youtube.com/watch?v=Iwpi1Lm6dFo

Schramm, W. (1955). The Process of Communication. In *The Process and Effects of Mass Communication* (pp. 3–26).

Samovar, L. A., & Porter, R. E. (1988). *Intercultural communication: A reader.* Belmont, CA: Wadsworth Pub. Co.

Shannon, C. E. (2001). A mathematical theory of communication. *ACM SIGMOBILE Mobile Computing and Communications Review*, 5(1), 3. https://doi.org/10.1145/584091.584093

Sloan, N. L., Ahmed, S., Anderson, G. C., & Moore, E. (2011, April). Comment on: "Kangaroo mother care" to prevent neonatal deaths due to pre-term birth complications. *International Journal of Epidemiology.* https://doi.org/10.1093/ije/dyq174

Strunk, W., & White, E. B. (1960). The Elements of Style. *College Composition and Communication, 11*(2), 121. https://doi.org/10.2307/355984

Suman Rao, P. N., Udani, R., Nanavati, R., Suman, R. P. N., Udani, R., & Nanavati, R. (2008). Kangaroo mother care for low birth weight infants: A randomized controlled trial. *Indian Pediatrics*, *45*(1), 17–23. Retrieved from http://www.scopus.com/inward/record.url?eid=2-s2.0-38349017067&partnerID=40&md5=4bc6c5f351989b338a1375bf1a8a32fe

Tracy, B. (2012, October 5). 3 Ways to Improve Your Communication Skills [Video file]. Retrieved August 8, 2018 from https://www.youtube.com/watch?v=D5hMN_XkPQA

Vinson, A. (2014, December 16). Why the color of your suit matters. Retrieved August 8, 2018 from https://www.bizjournals.com/bizjournals/how-to/growth-strategies/2014/12/why-the-color-of-your-suit-matters.html

CPSIA information can be obtained
at www.ICGtesting.com
Printed in the USA
LVHW061333200723
752936LV00008B/25

9 781516 52974